I0830025

TEEN WAR ZONE ©

Parents get your own back !

BRYAN SIDDERS

authorHOUSE

AuthorHouse™ UK
1663 Liberty Drive
Bloomington, IN 47403 USA
www.authorhouse.co.uk
Phone: UK TFN: 0800 0148641 (Toll Free inside the UK)
*   UK Local: (02) 0369 56322 (+44 20 3695 6322 from outside the UK)*

Published by AuthorHouse 01/12/2023

ISBN: 978-1-7283-9319-3 (sc)
ISBN: 978-1-7283-9320-9 (hc)
ISBN: 978-1-7283-9318-6 (e)

Print information available on the last page.

Any people depicted in stock imagery provided by Getty Images are models, and such images are being used for illustrative purposes only.
Certain stock imagery © Getty Images.

This book is printed on acid-free paper.

Because of the dynamic nature of the Internet, any web addresses or links contained in this book may have changed since publication and may no longer be valid. The views expressed in this work are solely those of the author and do not necessarily reflect the views of the publisher, and the publisher hereby disclaims any responsibility for them.

A must read for every Parent with Teenagers, or approaching Teens!
This is a family reference book, not a novel.

CONTENTS

CHAPTER 1

Introduction

This book is not written in novel form, although there are some good and interesting story lines and testimonials included as real examples referred to from true life experiences – to add spice to the reading and credibility to the information. It is more in statement format for quick easy reading – and indexed sub headings to help you find parts easier, and because it is intended to be a reference book – where you can go back again and again - to a section or subject, for some insight. It is unambiguous, straight forward and explicit. It is written in simple - Basic English language – so all can understand – even a Teenager reading the Book.

Tired	Dad is nowhere to be found.
Exhausted	No peace in the Home – or our minds.
Frustrated	I just want out.
At your wits end	Running on Empty.
Tried everything	Nowhere to go.
Don't know where to turn	Screaming and shouting abounds.
Can't control the Children	Guilt
No more energy	Pressure and Stress
Can't cope	That dreaded "G" factor – Oh my! He's Gay

If you are experiencing any of the above – you definitely have a Teenager! – join the Club!

This book has not been written by a Therapist, Physiologist, or any other professional, but by a regular parent, with the one unique advantage – I have had a whole series of Teens, one set after another, over about 30 years. This has more than qualified me to write this Parent Manual through the huge learning curve the Teens have taken me through – yes all the good, the bad and the ugly!

I have also done many years of counseling, of married couples, Families and mostly Teenage Boys.

This has been with Church, Welfare Societies, State Welfare, Schools, the Courts, Army, Welfare Homes, places of safety for children, and casual – off the street encounters – as it were.

I thank God for all I have learned, in spite of the nightmare struggle over the years, all the heartbreak and pain this has taken me through, and for how much this has taught me and matured me. I am so grateful for this invaluable knowledge I now have, to understand and be able to relate to youth in a wonderful personal and even intimate way. This is a really invaluable gift and treasure.

The good news is that it can easily all end in good! No matter how bad your situation in the home at present.

Do you have a Teen Angel – or a tyrant?

Unfortunately, with the first set – or with only one set of Teens, we usually only know what we did wrong when they get past their Teens – and then it's usually too late, unless we have another set on the way.

We should learn it all with the next one – but no – we can't, as we were so in the dark on the first one, we still did not learn the right approach yet! There will still be many lessons to learn.

And then the next one is a totally different character and personality anyway – so where to from here!

Back to this manual – keep reading, it will change your life! There is light, there is hope !

I would also like to caution Parents that this book has some stories that are very explicit, or raw. These are however true life issues that have happened in families with their children, even though some may seem shocking. But they are rich with true life events. Facing realities is a first step.

Furthermore, it's important to understand that although I am discussing the issues mainly around adolescents, yet it's imperative to appreciate that the sooner you start applying all the advice in the Book, the sooner you will correct your child's behavior, and even avoid the worst of the Teens years. It is never too soon to start with your child, they are never too young.

So this Book is also good for parents with young children.

My approach in this book may also seem harsh on Parents – this is not really intended, but rather to reinforce the message, because it is so important, and to get the point across of how much we as Parents need to change our behavior, before we can correct our Children. Please carry on reading, even if you are feeling bad that some of it may be your fault. You will soon read how many mistakes I also made along the way. Bringing up children is very difficult. We all make mistakes in this process. The very purpose of this Book is to expose our mistakes as Parents, so that we can adjust, before it's too late, before we lose our Child. This is to encourage you, by showing you how to cope.

We can't just throw our child away because it's proving too difficult, or because we don't know what to do, how to handle them, and are making so many mistakes. No problem, you are the average Parent, that's why you need to read this Book, to see how to change yourselves, to change our home environment, and restore a good family life for all in the home.

Most of my experiences have been with Teenage Boys, however, I have no doubt most of the principles apply to all your Children. As my stories are all about boys, I must use the male gender, but for no other reason than that they were boys.

This may be a good place to introduce my Poems – as they are mainly about life, emotions and relationships.

I will take the liberty to interject with a Poem from time to time, when it seems relevant, or that the Poem will bring further enlightenment to my expression.

I can't solve all your problems with your adolescent, but I can help you make a change and start to cope better. I can help with some very practical guidelines to help you navigate out of the dark.

Are you prepared to make some change?

Are you prepared enough to change enough to save your child, family and home?

I can help you to get your own back! The joy and peace of winning your Child back will bring you lifelong dividends of incalculable value and pleasure, whilst also setting the platform for him to launch into a more successful, happy fulfilled life – into more mature manhood, and eventually into better fatherhood.

So it's worth every effort you can make.

I Published my Book of Poems after some very stressful and particularly difficult Teenagers, and struggles in my own life and character.

The book is called "Glimpses of Life" Poems, Sonnets and Prose.

This first Poem perhaps explains what I am trying to do with this Book. It's for your sake, or at least the sake of your Teenager!

PURPOSE

There is no ill intent
upon you meant
or to impose
with my prose
and not to please
but to provoke
I will invoke
by all means,
to make you think
is what I mean.

CHAPTER 2

Get Your Home Back

It has been such a long hard struggle – it's too late, the damage is done – it can't be redeemed! Surely I can't get my child back? All peace has gone out the home – chaos reigns.

Yes it is a battleground, and yes you can get your home B A C K – if you will just persevere! Strive to get your OWN back – your child is worth it.

If you will make a decision to commit to making a stand – and stick to it – you will win! Your determination and commitment is what you need most to conquer the barriers.

2.1 Starts with a mindset change.

It all starts with you with a mindset change! Obviously, most what you are doing now is NOT working. You are the Adult, you must be in control of not only your child, but also yourself. You have to take control, get you mind, peace and home back.

Get your child back!

They are actually crying inside for you, for you in the way THEY need, not the way you perceive you need to be!

The outbursts and rebellion are normal behavior – and continue unabated – until you the Parent make a stand, lay down the House Rules, and then no compromise – until they earn favors, one by one, as they prove to be more obedient, more reasonable, more responsible.

They need to earn what they want through good behavior. If you are rewarding or still giving Pocket money etc to your child, with bad behavior unchecked, you are reinforcing the wrong, and indeed, you are perpetuating the problem.

You cannot reward bad behavior and still expect all to be well! Your actions are inadvertently giving off a message that their bad behavior is ok ! This actually confuses them and makes everything worse.

Don't be disheartened if it seems overwhelming. Or too much for you to take on. It's worth it all, as you will have such a wonderful home and family life again. Bring some fun back into the house, life is serious enough, without making it worse by a prolonged struggle for control. Your own mindset change may be the hardest part. I got peace and harmony at home, and from then on it was quite easy to maintain, as long as I was consistent in managing the pack.

CHAPTER 3

It's All Your Fault

Yes Parent it is!

Life has suddenly become more than difficult – it seems impossible! Around Puberty he just became a monster! He was always such a nice Child up till then, what happened?

The truth is – most Parents can't cope and need help! This is by no means an unusual situation. It's very common all over.

Once we come to the point of understanding and accepting this fact – we transcend the battle!

This is the most shocking truth to face before you can even start.

But it is not a fault of blame – but rather of ignorance – we are really not properly prepared in any way for the Teen explosion that is inevitable in the average home!

Although it's our fault, this book in no way is dealing with the guilt or blame for failure, but rather to provide direction for the way out. Feeling bad or carrying guilt will not solve anything, and may even hamper your efforts. If you feel bad, tell him, say you are going to change, and that he needs to give you a chance. Get past the guilt and shame, and get on with the programme.

The sooner we start this process of confronting ourselves, accepting the reality – then the sooner we can start to tackle the problem, and make the necessary changes.

No - it's not all over then, but we have started to gain control, we can then manage the Teen terror into a "Teen Angel" – as they say (or as we hope).

Yes, it really is our fault – because all children come into the world with a clear 'hard drive'. All our inputs, the environment and our actions start forming the basis for the way the child is going to respond to us and the world around them.

An aware mother informed me how it starts right from breast-feeding – who is in control? does the Baby get what he wants when he wants – or does the Mother start managing the process to more practical control of feeding - and not just letting Baby have his own way?

All too often Mom gives in to the cries to feed, often just to keep the peace – but this is fatal! This is a mere Baby but who's demands are only and selfishly for the NOW (of course because they know nothing else) – which only become more incessant and more demanding as Baby wins, and this is the pattern already set for the Child's demands and control, and then into Adolescence, where it's much harder to correct, because the pattern has been wrong for so long.

3.1 Puberty

Somewhere between 11 and 14 all Hell breaks loose! What went wrong – where did this monster come from?

He was always such a nice pleasant child! Now he's a terror. A tyrant. What changed. But again, you are the Parent, you are required to be the Adult (they actually expect that) and so you must take control, but through quiet and firm confidence, not through shouting, screaming and erratic demands.

Teens have a keen sense of what's fair, and judge you according to that standard – the more unfair you are, the more they don't respond. This is a critical issue – they have a fine intuition operating – so have accurate insight, even without necessarily having any understanding in the matter.

The Parent has to become the rational – firm, consistent but fair Adult – who is obviously in control.

Yes - puberty happened and everything changed. You don't understand him anymore, well, he doesn't even understand himself. That's why you have to become the Adult – the Parent, the control authority.

Your Teen is desperate for you to be their Parent, to be the Adult, the one they can talk to about anything – the one they can trust - but you have to win them over first. They are all looking to you for the needed guidance and direction they need – and when you can't provide it – they know and lose respect.

Otherwise who else will guide and lead him into adulthood?

Can your Teen trust you? Do your actions cultivate trust? Are you even approachable when he needs you?

Or just too busy!

There is no need to get despondent about the process to correct the situation with your child/Teen, and in the home! It really is not so hard once you make the decision and start to bring change for order. Thereafter you will have so much more peace in the home, such a better relationship, and such a pleasant home environment – that you yourself will be amazed.

It is just so much nicer when everyone is talking to everyone, in civil tones, and can actually start to have constructive relationships, and fun at home.

3.2 A perfect example is my Dogs

A perfect example is my dogs. A few years ago I got two new dogs, both huge Boer-Bulls, a brother and sister, one year old. The neighbor used to let them run out on the street, and applied no discipline, although they were obviously beautiful dogs. After getting fed up enough to go over and speak to her, I told her to stop letting the dogs wander the streets, as they are likely to get run over, and are a disturbance on the roads. She was not interested in any work or training to stop them, and simply retorted that she did not want them anyway.

I immediately offered to take them both – she was quite taken aback, and I think agreed more due to surprise, and not knowing what to do or say, rather than really wanting to give them to me.

I went to the back, got their beds and chains (yes they were tied up most of the day) and off I went with them in the back of my Bakkie (small covered truck).

I immediately taught them not to go out the Gate, and of course never let them go through, even if I wanted to take them out for a walk or anything, without first putting them on the leash – this was so I was consistent. I could not teach and discipline them if I told them not to go through the Gate if open, then on another day I opened the gate and took them through? how could they possibly learn what I wanted.

This is exactly the same with children, when we are teaching them – maintain consistency not to confuse them.

I only took me a few sessions, and less than 30 minutes in total to teach them NOT to go through the gate if it was open. This was obviously a well worthwhile effort, as it made the dogs safe, and they would now not disturb the roads and neighborhood anymore.

Unfortunately, however, I had not been watching The Dog Whisperer on TV yet, so did not know much more beyond basic discipline, like making them sit for their food before they were allowed to touch it, which also only took me no more than two sessions.

But the two started to fight, and I mean serious fighting, where the female was trying to dominate the bigger male, and seemed determined to kill him in the process.

I did not know anything about Pack Leader, etc, so although all the warning signs had started a while ago, and had been growing more frequent, I was totally unprepared for what to do, or how to avoid the problem.

Once again, this is exactly the same with children, hence this Book, or manual.

She tried to really kill him one day, and I spent 30 to 40 minutes trying in vain to separate the two dogs, which I did not succeed in doing – and in fact I was rather foolish as I could have been bitten very badly. She did not have a scratch on her, but he was very badly torn up all over the place, especially his legs and even one foot was torn open. Fortunately I had a choke chain on him so she could not bite his neck. He was at the Vet for several days and it took weeks of nursing him in confinement – until he was well again.

What I should have done was actually quite simple, I should never have let her aggression escalate. I should have taken control, I should have been the pack leader. I should have kept her in a calm submissive state, and it would have been quite easy as there was no aggression in her when she came. I was the problem, but I only understand this now after learning from Cesar Millan on TV. It amazes me now that my dogs KNEW I was not being the pack leader, they knew I was not controlling them, so she tried to take control.

And so it has been with our children and Teenagers, where we did not know what to do, they sensed it intuitively, they tried to take control, and so they got out of hand in no time.

NOTE – it is not about being a perfect Parent, and always doing everything correctly – but it is important to be committed, and to be consistent, and to be honest about what you are doing with them (as they know whats going on anyway – instinctively.

But here is the beautiful end to this story. I am definitely the pack leader at home now, and all the dogs know it, and respect me, and so now they can love me and are distinctly happier now. We have peace among all of them at home, they know the rules, I no longer have any difficulties with them, I don't even have to be hard on them, or train or discipline them anymore. It's just so nice and so easy now, and beyond keeping consistency and some maintenance now, there is so much more pleasure from them and no more problems.

It is like this with our adolescents – exactly the same. It's only difficult at first, then once we have the turnaround, it's wonderful for everyone, everyone knows their roles etc, and everyone's much happier. They are happier because they feel more secure – knowing you are taking control, are being the Parent – the Adult, The Pack Leader. This instills confidence in them and they calm down. Now I can really enjoy my pets more than I have ever been able to do all my life. Why are they happier now that they are disciplined, what's the connection? well because now they know where they stand, and know what they have to do and must not do, so now they feel more secure. This avoids the rebellion which comes out of them trying to take control – but don't know how to.

This is what brings peace and happiness into the home, rather than chaos – from the kids or the animals.

So, yes you can do it, and yes it is worthwhile.

CHAPTER 4

Why me?

I love my Child, why does he hate me!, why has this happened. We have a good Home, and are good loving Parents? We provide all his needs?

This has little to do with it. Teen War rages in every type of home around the Country, World in fact! The most common factor is the fact that they are a Teenager! Most of the other issues and problems are also fairly consistent.

A Teenager has many personal struggles. So much is new to him as his body changes, as he becomes much more awake and aware, self aware. As he strives to establish himself, to establish his independence. This is a normal and natural process. He is in transition to Adulthood, and it's very traumatic. On his own he has no point of reference, no one to help him understand, help him prepare, help him cope. His very inner drive for independence is contrary to all this, so of course he is confused, and in his confusion lashes out at the people closest to him, usually his Family. He is seeking and is desperate for guidance, and this is when he really needs his father. But the reality is that dad is not always around.

A Teenager is usually lost, insecure, full of physical changes they don't understand, his sexuality is emerging, it's all quite frightening and he is fighting to fit in – conform to the other Teens image – to be accepted. Peer pressure today is terrible, and Parents needs to understand it and cultivate enough confidence and security in your Child not to succumb to all the peer pressure so much – and won't need to if they feel right, feel accepted, feel understood, feel cared for. They need to know they can trust their Parent for direction and guidance when they need it. If he asks questions you can answer – tell him you don't know – but will find out. Try a search on the Internet – together, or seek more professional advice if needed, then feed back to him when you have it.

By both admitting you did not know the answer, and finding out and coming back to him will build trust & confidence in you. He does not expect you to know everything, or to be perfect, he expects you to help him when he needs it – and to do whatever it takes to achieve that.

4.1 Lost

Their emotions are running wild, and who can they go to? It has to be you. You must "get your own back", get your own Child back – don't leave them out there vulnerable and lost. They will hardly ever admit to being lost, or especially vulnerable – that would not be cool! In fact they are too insecure, too unsure of themselves to admit vulnerability, as that's not macho for the Boys, and can't admit it because then they would have to try deal with it all – which they instinctively know they can't – that's why they need you so much, even though they seem to be rejecting you and rebelling against you.

It's not actually you they are rebelling against, but how you are treating them, if they can't come to the one person they should really trust, should really be able to express their fears and doubts to – then who can they go to. Keep in confidence anything he tells you. If your ever repeat it, and it gets back to him he may never tell you anything in confidence again. That's exactly why they feel lost – because, deep down inside most are actually looking, hoping you will come through for them. You owe it to them to come through for them. They expect you to come through for them, so don't allow yourself to get pushed away by all the abusive rhetoric – that's just a veil, a mask – just their way of trying to cope. Yes of course it's completely the wrong way, but they don't know any other way yet – they don't know the right way yet. What way have you shown them? what has been the model for the last few informative years? have you been open, consistent, trustworthy – there for them, no matter what. Or have you been too busy with your career, or self justification of "earning" so you can provide for them like a good Parent

A Teen needs you more than any provision. They have an overwhelming sense of need of you for them in their crisis. They need you to be approachable – when they are ready, not when you are finished your work. Later never comes for them. They withdraw if not attended to at the time of their need. Not responding when they need you is emotional deprivation for them. Their perception is that you are NOT there for them, therefore they conclude you do not care!. Of course you care, you are doing everything you know how to prove you care, but none of those counts. All that counts is only that you respond to them and their need, as and when they need you. All their perceptions of your loving and caring from them are formed almost exclusively on your responses to when they need you, and how you do or don't respond to that. Openness and honesty is the absoloute key – and of course exactly when they need you – not later.

Even the structured environment is part of that need. They need you to have set the boundaries so that they are controlled by the limits – when they needed the limit to be there. Otherwise they feel lost, and sense you are not being a good Parent. That's where the insecurity and ultimate rebellion is birthed.

4.2 …is to feel cared for.

The ONLY person a TEEN can confide in is to one they sense CARES for them. Listen carefully Parent – a Teens most basic need – that is hardly ever fulfilled, is to feel cared for. Not loved or provided for – but cared for! This distinction is absolutely critical. Your care, demonstrated on a consistent, rational, firm basis will win over the confidence of your Teen, and will take all the hurt, mistrust, pressure and stress out of the relationship.

He's not expecting you to be perfect, he's not expecting you to get it right all the time – he's just expecting you to be open and honest about everything, and be there for him – to help him through this – just by having someone – an authority figure – that he can trust and confide in. He needs to talk, he has so many questions.

His peers cannot answer these questions, and if they do they are mostly misguided and so wrong for him anyway.

But I do love my Child? However, do you even realize that being nice and "loving" is going to destroy your Child if not matched with discipline and boundaries etc.

Giving him everything he wants, including his own way, is not love!
Watch the Film 'Miracle Worker', 1962 with Anne Bancroft.

This is a true story of a Mother who "loved" her young Daughter so much, she drove her to become mute! You are creating a Monster – who will be a juvenile delinquent as a Teenager, and if unchecked, will become a rebel at school, then at work, will not respect his Employer, and will have the same and indeed growing rebellious attitude to all community authority! including ultimately a total disregard for law and order, and will inevitably end up in conflict with the Police! All this will also keep him from respecting God as an authority's figure, which may then lead to spiritual problems as well.

This is what a Parent who LOVES their Child, but does not manage his Teen crisis, can create. Why me? because you have had the greatest influence over forming his character and personality during the critical informative years. Should you feel guilty and bad – no – it's too late for that. Go and honestly say sorry, and get on with learning how to relate to your Teen properly.

We have all been there, we have all needed to do this.

Guilt will only incapacitate you, and will not make you a better Parent. Realizing what's wrong, and changing from now on will save your Teen. This is true no matter how late or how far the problem has gone. In most cases it can really be turned around when the Parent turns around with a genuine concern and caring and trying to find out where he's at, and what he needs you to do. Your change in attitude will bring a quick change in him. Your consistency is then critical to win him over. He must now learn he can trust you – not because suddenly you will be perfect, but because from now on you are going to interact with him in an open and honest way.

Remember, never forget, no matter how much he says he hates you, or rejects or resists you, he needs you more than anyone in the World, and he's testing to see how sincere you are, and have you really changed.

He wants to see if you are now really committed to him – and he will test this in several ways.

Your faults and mistakes do not destroy your Child, ignoring or denying them do. Be open and honest with your Teen, they will accept far more of your failures than you would ever expect. It's this openness or your admission of what you do wrong that does not undermine you, but rather makes you more real to him, and so much more acceptable. Your admissions of your ignorance or weaknesses helps him trust you more. This helps him respect you.

Most Parents act as though the opposite is true.

So, why me?

because you can do it!

CHAPTER 5

The Great Gap

If you have not made a connection with him BEFORE Teens hit, – the gap will soar into a massive impenetrable divide – or so it will seem.

The gap or explosion on reaching Teens can never be avoided totally in most homes, but it's adverse impact can be reduced dramatically.

Both Parent and Teen are misunderstanding everything – almost every word or line is confusion and frustration – producing anger, resentment and rebellion.

5.1 Mental Pictures

Mom asks for Flour, he asks what colour as the picture in his mind was a Yellow Daisy! FLOWER but the problem is both words are pronounced and sound the same! But she wants to bake – this is where most of the miscommunications begin – our words form our mental pictures, which are usually different pictures in the mind of each person having a conversation.

We need to check each other's pictures as the conversation progresses when we converse, especially with our Teens, to make sure we are both speaking about the same thing.

And Mom and Dad have to take control of this, to ensure better communications, and manage the process. A huge adjustment on the part of the Parent needs to take place. They, the Teen are too immature to make the necessary change without the Parents direction, not by screamed instructions, but by example of calm open interactive attitudes, that a Teen can respond to. A Teen needs a rational consistent Parent that they can trust and learn to understand how they will respond to different situations. Teens will even test their Parents from time to time on these very issues. For example, they will say something outrageous to test your reaction, and then present the real issue – which is much less severe or less serious. But they can only tell you the real story, if you are receptive.

For example, Jill comes home and says a Boy made her pregnant today ! She wants to gage how you react. If favourable – then she will open up and tell you more. Actually, he just tried to kiss her. But if you react to the first statement, she will close up totally and not discuss the matter further. A huge pity and loss to the Parnent and the Teen. What a lovely opportunity to get personal and offer some sound advice about how she can help to handle this Boy, or this kind of situation.

One of my first reactions will be to appreciate the personal interaction and invite her to bring him home to meet. This affirms her, and allows you much more opportunity to discuss him further – and indeed check him out when he does visit.

5.2 Don't' freak out

One of my greatest lessons ever learned was over a 15 year old Boy, Lourens, at home one Sunday afternoon. He had two friends staying over. I was in the bath and noticed all had gone quiet. When three Teenage boys are quite, something is usually up! That up is usually up to no good.

In my concern, I jumped out the bath and looked around the House with no luck. I went out, called, and got a sheepish answer 'yes'.

What are you doing I demanded – come here right now (all in the wrong tone as I was obviously presuming the worst, but had not even given them the opportunity to explain themselves yet)! Anyway, Lourens came up first with his hands behind his back. I asked, or rather hissed "what's going on"? nothing he retorted. "but why are you so quiet, what were you doing" nothing he reiterated. Then I demanded he show me what was in his hands. As he reluctantly brought his hands round to the front, yes you guessed right, my worst fears confirmed – there he was with a bottle of Beer in his hands!

Well – I screamed like a lunatic for about 30 minutes straight. I was furious and disappointed all at the same time. I must have sounded like a fish wife! the whole neighborhood must have heard me!

I was so angry I grabbed the bottle from him and threw it at his feet. Unfortunately, it smashed on the concrete paving – and pieces cut into his feet quite badly!

All this because I lost control. Do you think this was educational or was conducive to developing trust? When I asked him why he had not just told me the truth at the beginning – his answer shook me – and changed me forever since then.

"Because I knew you would just freak out" he said – wow – what an indictment. This taught me that I had to be approachable for them to tell me the truth. For your Teen to confide in you – you first have to prove you can handle the truth – no matter what it is they have done. You can't demand the truth, until you can handle the truth – and some truths are very very difficult to handle. One of the Boys went out and came back very late – and I finally found out he had been with a friend, and had gone to a sordid Gay Bar to get picked up by some older man, and paid for sex to get some money to buy alcohol. Is this the truth you want to hear?

Well, I promised Lourens that day I would never freak out again – and that I would ask and stay quiet. If it upset or enraged me, I promised to stay quiet until I can be rational about the matter, and be able to discuss it further with him. I had to create the right environment to allow them to open up to me. Otherwise how could they ever open up – and that was the most important thing I needed for them to be able to do – and for their own sake, and the sake of our relationship, and for a suitable environment for him to grow in, and for the sake of him having a comfortable home.

The Parent must be firm and consistent. Almost every and any Animal – even the most obscure, can be trained? How is this possible when we can't even talk to them? But we can establish a communication, which if simple and consistent – that the Animal understands – mainly through the calm consistency, then the Animal will adapt to the required behavior – So how much more our superior, far more intelligent Child!

Once again, we the Parent, not the child are usually wrong! They can't be wrong as they are dependent on us – and on us being the Adult for them, the Adult they need.

We are supposed to be the Adult – parental, leader – so we should lead, be the responsible one.

We need to change our attitude, and change our communication – down to a level they can understand and relate to – which can be different for every Child. Most of our communications alienate our children. We can't talk to a child the way we speak to another Adult. We have to relate to our Teens at their level.

We can't demand they respect us – they automatically will respect us when we are honest, firm, rational, caring and consistent – this is the only way they can have a barometer of themselves. They need a firm point of reference in their lives, a good role model, so that they can stabilize. They need something stable to check themselves against, to check their own understanding and behavior against. This is far better if it is the Parent. The role model in their lives. Far better than someone outside the Family.

And Dad, it has to be you. You are the authority figure in the house. Don't abdicate this to Mom, because you work hard and are too tired. Your Child is your priority if you want peace in the home, and for him to grow up properly. And for boys, this is even more important. Your adolescent boy needs you dad, much more than he needs Mom now.

Unfortunately, most Parents are not that person. Are not the Parent they need to be. Are you? Sometimes we have even created the problem.

If not, now's the time to make the change. Leave the past and failure behind, and get on with getting your own back.

And come on dad – we need your help!

CHAPTER 6

Who's the Boss?

Parents, you already know that your Child has been trying to take control since Birth!

Yes, it starts from the Cot. If you pamper the demand crying, you will fall victim to enslavement to serving every whim of your Baby, then child, then finally a very seriously difficult Teenager.

Once they are a Teen, it's much harder to remedy. Much harder to take control, and will result in more confusion and more rebellion – and a great struggle for control. It must start from the outset, with parents in control. The irony is that Children need control, they need boundaries, and they instinctively know this. They will actually test you by pushing the boundaries. They want to know if you care enough for them to stop them. To deal with their irresponsible behavior. If you don't check or correct them – two very bad things happen. They perceive you are not in control, and that terrifies them – because they can't control themselves, so who is going to help them. This increases their fears and feeds their insecurities.

Secondly, they sense you do not love, do not CARE for them – then they feel more lost, and get worse. Although they seem to rebel against all rules etc, yet if you don't enforce them, and show you are the Boss, they will become more rebellious – trying to force you to take control of them. Teens need you to take control, so they can feel more secure in all their confusion of starting to deal with adolescence – and every other experience and lesson that goes with starting to grow up.

6.1 They need you to set the House Rules.

The whole irony is that they need you to set and enforce the boundaries for their behavior. They need you to set the House Rules, and to enforce them so they know where they stand all the time.

These rules can be different per child. Some children are more responsible, so can earn more rights and privileges. As long as you are always fair, rational, and consistent, they will trust and obey much easier.

Remember, it is critical to set rules you can keep – that you can enforce. It's a waste of time to set a rule that you can't enforce, or that is unfair and unreasonable. You will just undermine yourself if you do this.

6.2 Set rules you can keep.

My Mother was very wise when she discovered a packet of Texan Cigarettes in my Cupboard when I was all big and grown up at 14. She did NOT threaten me and tell me I could not smoke. How would she even know if I smoked with my friends in the afternoon in the bush? How could she enforce that?

She merely said Texan were strong and so not good for me, and immediately set a rule – "NO smoking in the House" See how clever that was. Because she would then both know about it, and be able to enforce the rule by stopping me if I tried to smoke in the house. Of course I was so deflated by actually not having been told not to smoke, that I did not bother after that. Well done Mom!

If you make Rules that have no purpose, or are unfair, or can't be enforced, you just undermine yourself as Parent, the authority figure, and perpetuate the Teen War!

CHAPTER 7

Communications

Yes, change your vocabulary – he does not even understand most of your words, let alone obeying them! Teens don't listen to most Parents because they are tired of all the shouting. They actually shut out your voice. It's not so much the volume as "that tone" !

How can he receive a high pitched shrill from frustrated Mom? How can he obey what he does not understand? The responsibility for conveying the correct communication is the responsibility of the Parent! Or the communicator. This means, when a Parent wants to tell their Teen something – they need to ensure they choose the moment to have maximum attention (i.e. not a screamed instruction during his favorite Sport game on TV – just when his team is scoring!) And that is already too late to tell him he should not be watching TV at this moment? This routine should have been established long ago – with agreement between both Parties as to when they can and can't watch TV? These arrangements, that the Teen also has to agree to is part of the process that brings peace and order to the home, and avoids all the fire fighting and yelling of why they are not listening to you? Who would listen in the same circumstances – certainly no other sensible adult would, so why do you expect your Adolescent Teen to listen? Would you listen to yourself when you shout?

All communications need to be rational, simple and clear – especially instructions, which must be arranged, communicated and agreed with well ahead of the event! You must solicit their agreement to any instruction or requirement, and make them accountable – by having an adverse consequence if they do not conform.

The more you come down on him for this and that, the more he will resist – if you have not given clear instruction first, and made sure he understood and agreed. The more you plan and arrange ahead of time – and get his consent, the more they will comply, and quite happily – because everyone understands the arrangement, it is clear what is required of the Teen, and it is also clear what the reward will be for compliance and obedience, and equally what the consequence will be for non compliance. Some sort of punishment or denial of something they want. Not a fight, as that will not work long term. Just an imposition or enforcement by the Parent of the consequence of the Teen NOT doing what he was asked to do, and that he even agreed to.

A Parent never wins a fight. The Teen already disrespects that you have lost control.

All this assumes the event was able to be planned ahead. In situations where there is a sudden demand for a request from the Parent, the way the Parent approaches the Teen will make all the difference. Rationalize with him, explain the situation and need, request assistance – not scream and demand action – which will only get a negative response anyway!

The better your usual communications are, the better the Teen will handle ALL of the routine requests, even the ones that come out of norm.

CHAPTER 8

What does he want?

Change your vocabulary and listen!

He will test your attitude to see if he can talk – will you freak out! Or stay calm, and let him unwind, then start expressing – once he is sure the environment, your attitude - is safe!

By testing you I mean he is liable to walk in and say he has made a girl pregnant – to test your reaction, then he will come to the real issue that a girl asked him for sex today. Do you see the trend? But he will only come to the real point if you accepted his fleece or probe and stayed calm and receptive to what he really wants to say.

A younger boy may rush in and ask for R100 cash right now. Then when you are calm, he will admit he really only needs R20 to take to School tomorrow, because they are all giving a friend a present. You must be sensitive to his approach – what has he really come for?

More than anything in the World your Teens needs and wants you!

Once he has you, and your attention, then he will always let you know what he really wants.

The circumstances, and the whole Home environment may indicate otherwise. His attitude may indicate otherwise. His apparent resistance to rule and order, his rejection and keeping away from you may indicate otherwise, but deep down inside, he wants and needs you. This is the one sure thing you can hold onto through all the time and trouble and struggle it takes to reach him, to get him back – is that he wants and needs you.

But he wants and needs you to be his Parent. To care for, and manage and control him properly, in a way that meets his needs – not lets him have his own way. You have to become the authority figure he needs. But not in an aggressive way, but rather in a calm, but firm and consistent way. He wants you to set up the boundaries. He wants you to set the standards, home rules that you must enforce if he is to respect you.

He can't do this – he desperately depends on you doing this. Then when he sees the Adult operating, he will respond positively – as he feels less confused and more secure – knowing you are really there for him.

8.1 Parents need to be more assertive and less aggressive.

Assertion is doing the right thing, in the right way, at the right time and for the right reason.

No need to explain aggression – which only engenders fear – and has no long term correctional impact.

So the trick is don't set up unfair or impossible rules. Start on a broader bases, with limited controls of what you can enforce, things or issues that are really good for him and the Family, and that is not unfair. Not rules for rules sake. He must also have some tasks or responsibilities in the Home. Mom can't do it all.

You must set these rules with his participation, understanding and agreement – then they will comply.

As you gain control, you can increase the rules, or set a stricter boundary.

He wants you to take control. He wants you to show him, indeed prove you care for him. Yes, that you care enough to see past his offensive attitude and all his nonsense, to start doing the right things yourself, for his sake and that of the Home and for the rest of the Family that has been so disrupted by his anger and resentment.

Most of his anger is against his perceived injustice of how his Parents are handling him. He instinctively knows you are wrong, even if he can't understand or define how or where or in what way – but he knows!

You can only combat this aspect by starting to be honest about your own ignorance and failings etc. He can handle all your shortcomings that you are prepared to admit to.

He cannot cope with your hypocrisy or unfairness.

Don't play mind games with your child! You will lose the game, the battle or even your Child.

OK mom, we all know this won't work!

CHAPTER 9

Care

Your Teen, and in fact even your younger child will always understand much more than you realize – instinctively. They know exactly what is going on and are masters at manipulating between the Parents to arrange to consciously get what they want. This is why Parents must stand together in agreement – especially in front of the Teen.

Discuss issues together – both Parents with him to stop him manipulating one against the other. Show him you both really care for him, and what's best for him, even when he does not agree or like what's best for him at times. When there are Brothers and Sisters, he has to be made to consider them also – everyone has equal rights in the home. Yes certain privileges can be earned by work or good behavior – to earn favors etc., as the teens proves co-operative and obedient and responsible. This is not necessarily age related, but rather attitude related. At times a younger Brother or Sister can earn better and more privileges than an older Brother – but as long as you Parents are consistent in how you deal with this, and how you let them earn favors etc – then he will see the fairness and adjust accordingly.

Do you realize that your Child knows they have to go to School, and if you had to let them off, this would cause a deep mistrust in the child, that will be difficult to correct. So it is with almost everything else. He knows what's right and best for him, but will try to resist – partly to test if you really care enough for him to enforce what he knows he needs. He does not feel he has any other way to test you - to see if you really care for him. Saying you love him solicits very little by way of making him feel safe and secure. (although he also needs that) You have to show him, prove to him, demonstrate that you love him, and you can best do this through consistent care, always trying to do what's best and right for him and the Family. Then, in this environment saying you love him becomes a reassuring affirmation, that is really meaningful. You must bring balance to the whole family. You cannot allow him to dominate any aspect, and you cannot allow him to demand more than you can or want to give, or more than the others are getting.

CHAPTER 10

Discipline

A Child instinctively needs discipline to feel secure. In fact, in a home with no discipline, the Child feels unloved and not cared for – and this leads to gross insecurities, unhappiness and rebellion is the outcome of his expression of his frustration and anger. (even when he does not understand why). This is why we have been created with family structures, and Parents who are responsible to "bring up a child in the right way, and he will not depart from it" as it says in Proverbs 22.

The amazing thing is that this is even true of Adults, only to a lesser degree – depending on their maturity and responsibility levels. Most Adults needs boundaries and limits so they know where they stand, imagine an Office with no rules? it would be chaos – everyone doing their own thing,

Without discipline and structure and indeed even certain routine in the home, the Teen is lost and will soon show it. Discipline, and indeed even structure and routine, helps bring some order to all the confusion he feels and is experiencing. His body is changing rapidly, his emotions are running wild, most of them little understood by him. This is why he needs his Parents so desperately at this time especially. He needs someone he can lean on, and look up to. He needs direction.

Most Parents don't like punishment. But it's not about punishment, it's about discipline and control.

Well, indeed, this may be a little too harsh!

Discipline is achieved by setting up the House Rules, making them clear, getting your Teen to agree to the rules as being fair and reasonable and necessary. You can bargain for acceptance by having a reward system for compliance, and then demerits for breaking the rules. These all need to be spelt out – written out in fact, especially for younger children, or more difficult Teens. Until you write them out on a notice board in the house, he will always claim he did not understand or realize that's what you meant.

A Teen will find every industrious way to avoid the rules, and have every creative excuse for why he did not keep the rule – but there must be no compromise. Your Rules can allow for one, or maybe even two warnings over certain issues, but then you must impose the penalty, or the consequence of his actions. This is the best way to get an adjustment in his behavior. As soon as he sees you are serious, and that you yourself are maintaining the outcomes of the Rules, he will adjust and conform very quickly. The more you compromise, the more he will get away with, the harder it will be to bring control, peace and order.

Imagine a Country with an Army with no discipline? chaos would reign, and the Army could never be able to defend its Country or protect its Citizens. This is why when young men are drafted into the Army, or even when they volunteer, they go through ' induction course ' or Boot Camp - is the strictest possible discipline, with absolutely no compromise. Every Army in the world learnt this lesson centuries ago – to change the wrong mindset of the young man, in the quickest way possible, it is vital to impose the harshest possible discipline – with no excuses or way out allowed. The consequences are imposed rigorously. This shapes them into obedience and order very quickly, and they will never forget this training during their entire stint in the Army – no matter how many years they spend there.

This is not to suggest you convert your home into a military barracks– but it demonstrates the point and important role that discipline plays.

And laying out the house Rules makes it easier all round for everyone.

CHAPTER 11

Structure

He is insecure so fights to be right! When he fights, he is defending his position – his current level of understanding, which he can't break away from for fear of losing himself. It took me years and many practical experiences in different circumstances with many teens and many years to understand this.

I just wanted them to change their way of thinking and understanding, based on what I would say is right. But they cannot, until they feel they can trust you and your opinion. He will vehemently defend his own opinion, or position, or his current belief, because that is all he has to hold onto – to hold himself together with. He can't just let it all go, even if he is wrong. Even if he himself thinks he may be wrong, he can't change his opinion, or let his current view go untill he feels more secure, more safe with you. So be careful about smashing his views or opinions. Take it easy, give time to learn what he really feels and believes. Slowly, as you gain his trust, start to give him more information, so he can review his position, but before you can get to that, you need to bring order, create the right safe environment. Bring control, and his compliance.

For now, he has to think or believe he knows everything, and that he is right; this is his way of coping. He believes he is right on all points. Indeed, if you are unable to set up some routine structures in your Home, you may also feel lost, or certainly out of control. It's only when he reaches about 20 to 22 that he realizes, or rather, admits his Parents knew more than he thought!

Your Teen needs rules and boundaries within which to operate. Without this, they keep stretching out and pushing you to try to find the limits. The boundaries are where you set the limits. It is irresponsible of any Parent to think the Teen should set his own boundaries, no matter how good or responsible the Teen may be.

It's your house, you make the rules, just like your boss does at work!

When you go to a new Job – the first thing you need to know is what are the rules of that establishment. What is the structure, who is the boss! Who do you report to, what time must you come to work, and finish etc. It's really that simple and just as necessary for your Teen in the Home! How on earth can they operate without these simple rules and structures – yet most Parents don't set up this structured environment, then wonder why they rebel, or in the least don't conform – why there is chaos in the home?

Until you set up the rules, they don't even know what they are expected to conform to.

They need to know what is required of them.

Well - for the same reason, there would be chaos at work if the cleaner tried to be the Boss, because the Boss was not doing his Job!

Structure brings order, and order makes it clear what's required, this then calms everyone down, and eventually brings peace in the home. In a structured environment, you will still get some problems or outbursts, but you will be able to deal with them much easier and quicker, as there is a structure in place that helps you know what to do and how and when to do it. This factor alone brings improved order.

The whole Universe has structure for order. A building has structure, otherwise it would just collapse. How then do we expect our Families not to collapse without structure.

Routine and rules are part of structure. Routine is very important to a child's security. You must build some level of routine into their daily lives. In fact, the younger they are the more important this is. Set the trend, start the structure, the young kids will be much more co-operative, life will be easier, and you will be happier.

This is very important for very young children, as it paves the way for avoiding the rebellious Teenager. Routine helps them to know what to expect, and so lowers the stress or pressure from uncertainty.

CHAPTER 12

Examples

PARENTS JUST DON'T UNDERSTAND

They give birth
but take away the life!
make a body
but deny the soul.
Love child!
should be – but alas
all their hate does not abate
all they want is to abuse
as they refuse
the little person to be.
Why can't they see
why can't they know
the child should be what the child knows!
Battered, abused, denied refused
one way or another
they only destroy
his beautiful life
this manifestation of them
what a pity, what a waste.

> Why can't they see
> why can't they know
> all the child wants
> is to be who he is.

Were they all a success? Did all the boys come right, and end up with a good outcome.

Mostly!

I have had from the very worst boys - to the best. From good and bad homes.

Welfare cases, suicide, gays, drug addicts, male prostitutes, prison cases, Teenage parents, abused cases (sexual, mental, emotional and physical) – and all this before age 17.

But then also boys with nothing wrong more than that they could no longer live with their Parents, and left home! How bad is that? How destitute must a boy be to leave home?

Abused boys, abandoned, unwanted and rejected, kicked out of Home. Uncared for, neglected. So they do the most unnatural thing, and leave what should be the safety and security of home and being with Parents who should want and care for them.

So I have had all types, from all backgrounds!

The greatest majority worked out well.

12.1 Lourens

I met him one lunch time during School Holidays. He was walking in Hillbrow, Johannesburg, with Danie (mentioned in this book) and another of their friends. They all three were a pitiful sight. Scruffy, dirty, and very badly dressed. Lourens, not Danie caught my attention that day, our eyes met and we connected. Focused attention is very important to a teenager. This tells them how interested you are in them. Eye contact is very important to your Child, and when backed up by physical contact is invaluable for him and for building his self-esteem. This is one of the best forms of affirmation you can give him. (at any age) If Parents are not touching their Teen, there is a problem, and this divide will grow unless corrected. I have that way of giving focused attention, of looking right into them, searching for a response – searching for light in all the apparent darkness and gloom of their lives.

I was immediately drawn to him by all the spark and life that I saw in him, in spite of the dreadful outward appearance. I also knew he had responded, but not outwardly. I tested my instincts by ignoring him. I was sure he would stop and allow my interaction. My sense of him was so strong, I needed to test this to make sure. So I still ignored him. He walked two blocks before mustering the courage to turn round and come back. I just stood looking into the shop window. My car was parked right there, but being a BMW, I did not want him to see my car before I had checked him out. I did not want him to come for anything material. He came back and walking straight up to me asked for some money for food! The rest of this story on Lourens can be read later.

12.2 Danie

For now I want to deal with Danie – his friend, whom he always brought with when he visited me (I suppose he felt safer not being alone – after all he had been used and abused so much – one couldn't blame him). Danie unfortunately was one of the very few that did not work out or come right. I gave him huge attention. I even had him assessed by a Psychologist – something I have never advocated or done again. There was something so basically wrong I could never quite put my finger on it. I took him into my home, got him through the last of his High School, got him a Job, bought him a car – but he never appreciated anything, and kept wanting more and more. He stole everything valuable out of my house to feed his drugs he was now taking more and more regularly. Very shortly he was a total drug addict. I was never able to help or correct this boy. In retrospect, I realize this was one of my earlier cases, and part of the problem was I had given him far too much. He came from a poverty stricken home, straight into my abundance, blessings and prosperity. I should have controlled this aspect much more. Should have made him work for and earn certain things he wanted. I always just bought what he asked for. After all, he had never had anything, and I wanted to give it all to him. FATAL!

Danie showed all the signs of this picture – and more:

12.3 Drugs

Why is this story in my book? Because of one simple truth – besides giving him too much to easily, drugs is so debilitating, that I have never seen any level of rehabilitation – once they are addicted. I say this by way of warning – of how serious the drugs issue is, but also because in all my experience, and with all the years of counseling, I have never been able to help a drug addict. No, not at any level.

I even joined "Tough Love" – a Worldwide Organization that handles drug addicts. I wanted to learn how I could help drug addicts; I could not understand why I could never reach them or bring any change or improvement into their lives? The first meeting was a total shock to me. They told me quite adamantly that I could NOT help a drug addict, and that I could only leave them till they hit rock bottom, then want help?

They counsel the Family more, to help them cope with the drug addiction in the Home.

Through bitter experiences, I have come to find this all to be true. So I do not even try help drug addict families anymore. I am not saying there is no help or no hope for them, I am only admitting this is not my forte, and so I leave it alone.

Back to affection and touching.

The importance of touching your Child, even when, or maybe especially when they are in their Teens, cannot be overemphasized. Being older does not mean they don't want to be touched anymore – they love it and need it.

12.4 Touching Mark opened his heart

Mark was a good example of the importance of just a touch – it turned out to be far more important this day than I could ever have expected.

I was at the Bus stop dropping off Lourens to go back to his reform School he was in at the time, when I got a call from the State Welfare Office. They were asking me if I would go and attend to a difficult case of a young Welfare Boy they had recently placed in a Foster Family, where they - and the family felt his Gay tendencies may affect or influence their own Teenage Son.

I arrived at the AFM Welfare Office in Elsburg, to be taken to Marks' adopted Home. His story was and remains the worst I have ever heard of or been involved with. He was fine, and had no problems other than being Gay, but he was well adjusted to this. He was in Welfare because his mother had handed him over at about 13 or 14. His older brother as a Teenager, has been sexually molesting Mark since Mark was very young. He could not say anything to his Parents, and basically did not really even understand what was going on. It was his own brother so it should be ok? or so he felt – until he arrived at puberty himself, then his own self awareness and his own sexuality made him feel this was not right what his Brother was doing to him, so he told his Parents. The Father was so horrified, and could not deal with this at any level at all, so he committed suicide. Then the Brother, now feeling so bad about all the problems he had caused in the Family also killed himself! The Mother, bereft of her Husband and older son, just copped out of it all. It was too overwhelming for her, so she chased young Mark out the house, and gave him over to Welfare, saying he was a bad Boy and blamed him for all the problems.

You can see for yourself he had nothing to do with the blame! But that was his circumstance when I arrived at his Foster Home to meet him and evaluate the situation to write a report of recommendation for Welfare of what to do with Mark now.

He was standing on the verandah, a very quiet sensitive 17 year old – I think in retrospect the lady of the house had already kicked him out, another rejection for him all over again.

When I met him, I discovered he only spoke Afrikaans, and me English – so we could not converse at all. As I approached him, I noticed all the cut marks – scars on both his wrists – evidence, token, mementos of his pain and low self-worth, and so he had tried several times to kill himself I instinctively took both his arms in my hands and asked how he could damage himself so badly when I would not even scratch the bonnet of my Car. I consciously wanted to relate to and share his private pain and struggle, and wanted what he had done to himself out in the open, to show I cared, wanted to know more, and that I accepted him exactly like that and for that, no matter what. I did not want this hidden or covered up. It had to be out in the open – and even though suicide is serious, I had to address it – indeed face it if I was going to be any help to him. We have to reach our children where they are at.

What I did not know at the time that proved an absolute breakthrough with him, was that I had touched him. He told me a long time later that he was so surprised when I held his arms. He said it went right to his heart and opened himself up to me totally. He was so deeply touched by me touching him, and here is what he told me as to why:

He said that in all the years of counseling he had received, from Family, Church, Welfare (both State and Church Welfare Workers) Foster Homes and foster parents,

NO ONE HAD EVER TOUCHED HIM!

He said everyone avoided touching him as though he had a plague or would contaminate them with something awful – so although they spoke to him, they never touched him, and consequently never ever reached him. I touched him and reached right into his heart and whole life immediately. What an amazing lesson for me. This had not come out of any book (although much later I did read about importance of touching in Dr Ross Campbells Book discussed elsewhere in this book). This was an instinctive reaction to how to approach Mark. I must thank God for a God given gift when dealing with these Teens, of how so many times I just do the right thing when I did not have any idea of what to do. I must also add that as you use your talents, gifts or whatever you want to call them, they do develop, and they do refine as you gain more experience, as it starts to just come naturally, even unconsciously – but they are always there at the fore when you need them.

12.5 Some other successful stories

I gave a lift to a young National Serviceman in Army uniform one afternoon near John Vorster Square. He must have been in the car with me for 30 to 45 minutes. As usual, I pried into him immediately to see where he was at. He blurted out all his problems, and I gave him some advice and my Card, as I usually do in case they want to contact me for more help. I heard no more of him, and thought no more of the incident. There was no major connection or interaction – or anything like that. I do not even recall what advice I gave him regarding his situation. However, many years later I got a phone call. I did not remember his name, but I did remember him because of his Uniform and being picked up near John Vorster Square. He just called to thank me to say that he took my advice and it had changed his whole life. That is reward – so much benefit for so little effort.

I have had other calls like this, years later, like from Nick, with the rich Father Businessman from a good well to do suburb here in South Africa.

I had Nick at my house a few Sunday afternoons at the request of his Father. I quickly found out what was really bothering him, and why he was being so otherwise. It was because he was in a Christian Home, but his Father did not think he was acting as he thought he should. He was a lovely boy, real nice nature, character and personality, but because his Father had caught him taking drugs with his friends, he told him he had the Devil in him, and that he was going to Hell. Of course this really bothered Nickdeeply, especially as he was also a Christian. This made him feel very guilty and bad. He was by no means a drug addict. He just did what many Teens did, and played around with some drugs.

Once I had identified what was bothering him so much, and showed him from his Bible that this was not the case at all, he did not have the Devil or even a Demon. God's grace is sufficient for all our sins and weaknesses, and if we ask forgiveness for anything, He does forgive us. Anyway, Nick was fine after that, and I no longer needed to see him anymore, although I had failed to reconcile his Father to him.

However, years later he also called me to say he was now happily married, and wanted to thank me for changing his life for him – in just those few short sessions. I had no idea I had had that much impact on him.

There are many more such stories, but here is one last one from John…. He ran away from Home and his Dad when he was 14. I took him in. Years later, after he already had a child of his own, he wrote me this letter, or this extract out of the letter which I just found again recently – inside one of my books I keep going back to. This is very precious to me because it's from his heart: "Bryan, The reason why I wanted to write this letter to you is because I wanted to truly thank you for everything you have done and that you are doing for me. I thank the Lord for letting you into my life for you have been much more to me than just a friend, you are like a Father to me and I think of you as my family. You are someone that I will keep in my life till the day I die. I just wanted to say thank you Bryan for your friendship and your guidance. You mean a lot to me and I believe I can say that I care and love you very much"

What beautiful words from a young man. These are what make it worthwhile. Not because I need to be stroked, but because it shows how much they have really been helped.

He did not write this letter because I am perfect or because I did everything right. No, he wrote this letter because I touched his heart, I reached out to him, to help him in his time of need, and to help put him on track.

So it is all worthwhile. It is worth it to save even one young life. These were not even my own flesh and blood; these were boys I just counseled, or took in, or who became my Foster kids. Yours' are most likely your own Children, your own Son yearning for you. Needing you. These are just some examples to show it is all well worthwhile.

CHAPTER 13

The Boundaries

Children, especially Teens need boundaries – so they know where they stand!

If there are no boundaries, no rules – what will be their point of reference to follow? How will they know when they are going wrong, even when they are right – when there are no boundaries – no fence, no limit to control his behavior.?

Have you seen the **Movie "The Beach" 2000 with Leonardo DiCaprio?** A bunch of young people thought they had found Paradise on this remote Island, and they decided to live there in peace and freedom! But human nature being what it is – there can be no Freedom, no peace without rules, regulation and structure to control and manage society – and surely it all begins in the Home as our Child is growing up. This Movie makes the point very well. It all ended in chaos.

What will really surprise Parents the most is that the Child not only NEEDS these boundaries, structure, rules and discipline, but deep down they want it – they know they don't understand enough to cope, so they NEED their Parents to take on the parental role properly, and not to abdicate, or delegate it back to the Child!

They can only feel comfortable, safe and secure, when they KNOW their Parents are in control. When they know what they can and can't do, when they know the limits of their behavior.

ALSO, when they conform they can feel safe secure and happy. Rewards for good behavior then reinforce all of this.

This obedience gives them a sense of security and satisfaction that they can't get in any other way. This is what will build their self esteem, and prepare them for the big wide world they are entering. If they don't have boundaries and rules to follow, they can't get this satisfaction – so they feel lost, and clamor for a way out. They become demanding, pushing for their own way – but really pushing the Parent to become the Parent they are supposed to be, the Parent the Child instinctively needs. The child experiences emotions of being lost, which then grows into insecurity – with many adverse expressions, all of which make the problem worse. All this leads into rebellion most of the time.

The Child actually experiences this from birth, but just to a lesser degree. Once they are an adolescent, they are struggling to understand themselves, are fighting to establish themselves, fighting to establish their identity and independence. This is a normal part of their growth to manhood. But they are now bigger and stronger, and more in a position to put up a fight with their Parents. Most of it is rhetoric. The shouting is demanding something be done. Demanding that the Parent take control. If they won't, then the Teen will try – but unfortunately, this does not work as the proper roles are reversed, and the Teen cannot take control and have a good outcome – that will bring disaster on the Family. There can't be two bosses in any environment, and certainly the Teen can't be Boss of the house – but he will resort to this if you the Parent are not taking, indeed forcing the Parental role of authority.

You the Parent obviously love your child very much, and also want the best for him – so these are guidelines to help you do that in a better way, that will be more effective, and in so doing release all the love in the Family.

13.1 Parents, it's your home.

All too often, the Parents forget it's their home and they are entitled to take control, entitled to make the rules. Alternatively, they lose sight of this in the throes of battle, but they need to get perspective, and not allow any Child to hi-jack their Home from them. This is exactly what happens in all too many cases. Why do we as Parents allow this. To allow a Child to subtly take control of an Adult is absurd. !

Peace at all costs is a lie, and does not work. The more you compromise for peace, the more you will pay later. To have a happy secure, well-balanced child, there must be a controlled environment in which he operates, and lives – so that he always knows what he can and can't do – what his modus operandi must be – as dictated by the Parent. His conformity is what makes him feel safe and secure, and that then makes him feel happy. This is the road to peace and that avoids the rebellion developing.

Yes, he will still take chances, and yes, he will still break the rules after you have achieved all this – however, this is now a totally different situation. Now you are dealing with the breed instinct, boys will be boys, and not a delinquent adolescent. Now the correction is simple and effective – and is not in any way detrimental to the structure, your control or his good healthy growth. He will take chances, knowing full well he will pay if caught, but all this is in good attitude, and with a clear simple being mischievous. Quite different from before, when all this began, quite different from the demon you were confronting for control, and he was resisting the struggle with all his might. Now he is just being a boy, and you need have no fear he is reverting to past bad behavior. He is now just being mischievous as Boys will be.

When you achieve this state, you will have real peace in the home. Now you can all live more normal lives, where you all share the Home equally – not dominated by the Teen Demon. Now love can be expressed and flow so much easier. This also allows affection and more intimate discussions around whats really going on with him. This is vital for him, and good for you. Being the Parent you need to be, and that he actually needs. Not a task master or his adversary.

Now he is just being a regular Teenage boy, full of energy, lust for life and zeal for everything. Now he is going to go for all the good clean fun he can have and get away with. And he will be very precious in your eyes.

He is no longer challenging you or your authority – that has already been clearly established.

Now he can enjoy being a boy, and now you can enjoy having this precious life, experimenting every day with everything – being a whole new person, developing into the best person he is supposed to be, and can be. Now you can contribute constructively in his progression from Boyhood to Manhood.

And each one of your Children will be different. Each will go through this easier or harder, quicker or longer, and each at a different level of intensity, depending on their own makeup, character and personality, or just their stubborn will, or impish ways.

Hopefully we are going to do a much better job at this than most of our Parents did. This Book will definitely help you achieve exactly that.

All of you, the whole family will be enriched by the experiences he takes you through!

CHAPTER 14

Children Copy Parents – Good or Bad

Children emulate their Parents, especially boys of their Father.

The smallest boy will watch his Dad, and even sit the same way, or shake his leg up and down in the same way. This is cute.

Unfortunately, however, boys will also emulate all their Dads bad ways or habits. So it's no good to hold a smoke in one hand, and a bottle of Beer in the other hand, while trying to explain to your child why he should not smoke cigarettes or drink alcohol! This simply does not work. Children do what you do - and not what you say. What Parents do forms an imprint on the young mind, and that picture is what becomes their standard – after all, that's all they have seen for years in too many cases, how can we then expect them to come out differently.

If Parents are living properly right in front of their growing child, everything will be easier as he grows into adolescence.

Jewish Families are among those cultures who keep a wonderful tradition, that sets such a good example and is followed generation after generation, as the boys emulate their fathers on Sabbath.

Every Friday night, after sunset and Shul, the whole family sit down to Sabbath dinner – together.

Even though not of the Jewish faith, I have had the wonderful privilege, through my many Jewish friends – to spend many a Friday evening going to Suhl then dinner with these families.

This is quite a unique and wonderful experience, and demonstrates why eating together is so important.

Parents, if you are not eating together regularly, this will cause more problems. Set the rule – everyone has dinner together, as often as possible. This brings the wonderful opportunity to all to express how your day went, what's going on with each of you, and you will soon see or hear what's troubling your child by your careful observations.

Set the right example for all to follow.

CHAPTER 15

Accountability and Consequence

We have to learn to teach and instruct our Children to become accountable, and this is an ongoing task.

Accountability means being responsible for their words and deeds. Accountability teaches them there is a consequence to their actions.

They can't just say and do what they want and get away with it.

If they do something wrong, and you correct them, then in a 'huff' or frustration they blurt out "then I won't eat my dinner" hold them to that. Do not under any circumstances allow them to eat their dinner that night. No, they will not die missing one meal, yes they will be hungry – but that is the very point, this is the consequence or outcome of their short temper.

It is also entirely their own fault, so do not feel guilty or bad. But, even if you do, you should still carry out the consequence.

This is how Children learn to be careful what they say, to consider their words carefully, makes them more respectful and will save them a lot of trouble down the road, right up into their job and marriage.

By setting this standard consistently, and every time, you bring about the desired change, and the right behavior, then by the time they are Teens, you won't have as many problems.

If they are already a Teen, and you are having this problem, all the more reason you must bring an immediate halt to this unacceptable behavior, and start making him accountable.

If he walks in and slams the door! ask him not to do that again, but you also need to give a consequence at the same time, so he knows if he does that again, he is going to pay! He must understand the terms before you can impose any discipline, as this is both fair, and also reasonable, and he will fully appreciate the situation, and will know it is his own fault if he does it again.

It is no good to scream at him "stop slamming the door"! Your behavior is equally unacceptable, and sets no rule, and makes no demand of him, and lays out no consequence for his action.

It is also no good to make wild or false accusations or threats, that you never would, or worse, never could carry out — as this dramatically undermines your own authority, and will never command respect from him.

For example, you cannot threaten to kill him the next time he does that! You can now see why this is useless and just exasperates the whole problem – everything just keeps getting worse as you yourself are breaking the rules. Don't make idle threats.

How can you possible expect him to listen to you, and especially to respect you regarding everything else in the Home and his life!

You the Parent have to bring the peace to the Home. You are the older, the Adult, and supposed to be the more responsible party to all this. You must make the change first, and start setting the right rules and standards, that you expect, and you keep them first, then he will follow.

CHAPTER 16

Anger

An angry Teenager is a very dangerous situation, because it is so volatile, and not always apparent!

Even worse, if it is suppressed, and turns to passive aggression. At worst this can lead to suicide. At best passive aggression causes many problems for people around them. They so are often up to no good, to get others back for what they feel has been done to them. This leads them to do very destructive things, from just small to large serious issues, like join a Gang where he can vent his anger and rage on others, or extreme cases to demonstrate where this can lead to, at worst they can become a terrorist, or at least join a Criminal Organization to vent their anger and hate.

Anger can make the Teenager, or even young man react to everything all the time. Whenever his buttons are pressed, mostly inadvertently, there is an almighty explosion. This constant volatility, this reaction to almost everything around him is a sign or good indication of anger. The family cannot walk around the house on tender hooks for fear of upsetting the Teen – this is not fair to everyone else, so this anger must be identified and addressed.

One of the best books written on this subject is by one of my other favorite **Authors – Dr Ross Campbell "How to really Love your Teenager"** A must read for every Parent with Teenagers, or children approaching adolescence. This is the very best work book, or manual for understanding Teenagers that I have ever read.

'The Road less travelled' will help you understand yourself, and 'How to really Love your Teenager' will help you to understand your Teenager. This book has a section on explaining what this anger is all about, that is unique in its simplicity and truth.

There is always a deeper underlying cause for anger. Often it is the injustice the Teen perceives of his Parent, or Parents. Being unfair to your child on a consistent basis will create this anger, that will erupt at some point, usually when he becomes a Teenager.

The Bible says that fathers should not provoke their Children to anger (Ephesians 6 vs 4) Very sound advice.

Neglect can also cause anger, Parents fighting all the time, picking on the kid unnecessarily, having a favorite Child and showing it. This breeds resentment, which then leads to anger if left unchecked.

Anger is not always easy to detect. You have to keep watchful eyes on your Teen, watch for mood or attitude changes, watch for out of the ordinary outbursts – try to see what prompted it. You will need to find the cause to address this problem.

A divorce can cause the Child to develop a deep fear (insecurity) or resentment, that can easily become hate – for the parent he is with, having caused the other Parent to be absent. This is of course misplaced, but it is his perception, so his reality.

Remember we all experience anger from time to time. So anger in a Teenager is not automatically wrong or bad, but what is the cause, and how does he deal with his anger. He will need help to direct the anger properly. He should not kick the dog, because his sister took his favorite piece of cake! You need to encourage him to identify his anger, and then try to direct it properly or appropriately.

If you can get to the main cause, and remedy the cause, the anger should dissipate.

16.1 Angry with Lourens

Here is an example of me being angry with something Lourens did, that justifiably made me angry - but how I dealt with it, and how I dealt with him at first was very important, as it needed to become a life changing lesson, rather than evoke anger or resentment in him.

I always have a small plastic packet of small change in my car for parking meters and tips etc. One Sunday afternoon, back in 1989, just after we left my house to go out, I noticed the money packet was not there! I thought for a moment to check that it should still be there, and in fact full, and that I had not given it away, or taken it out the car or anything like that. This is a very good process to take yourself through before reacting. Screaming unfairly at him – especially if he did not take it would break down many months of building our relationship and stabilizing him. (At this time he was still fairly new with me and was only 14, just approaching 15). I had to handle this carefully. First I had to be really sure, Secondly I had to give him the benefit of the doubt when I approached him, to allow him to defend himself, and also if he had done it, I owed him the opportunity to come clean – before I threatened or punished him in any way. I thought about it very carefully, and I was getting more and more angry as I drove, because I was more sure it had been there, and that in fact he had taken it. By now we were driving on the Highway (Freeway). I made my decision, I had to address this, I had to get it all out, otherwise it would be very difficult for me to trust him with anything, and if I could not trust him, I could not really help him much. I had to make a lesson of this to ensure I did it in the right way, so that he would know he could always tell me the truth, and so that he would know I would not punish him when he did tell me the truth. These are God given opportunities for all of us to learn.

My dilemma however, was how to achieve all this, and not make him feel the money was more important than he was – he himself! I knew he was more important than the money, to me it was all a matter of several principles. However, how to make sure I conveyed that properly so that he really knew and believed that I valued him much more than the money - was a critical issue to me.

So here is what I did, which turned out to be exactly the right thing to do, it must have been divine inspiration because I really did not know what to do beforehand. I stopped the car on the side of the Highway. I then told him about my money packet, and asked if he had taken it at all, which I said was no problem as he may have needed it, but said I needed him to ask me in future if he wanted money or anything, and that I would always give it if he needed it. I explained how important it was that I could trust him, and how I needed him to tell me the truth. He denied it – which increased my dilemma, and made me furious. I asked again and again in different ways, and said I knew for sure the money packet was there, because it was always there, and that I never took it out. He still denied it. However I knew by his body language etc. that he was lying, so now my dilemma was even worse. I now knew he had taken it, but he was not letting on. We were reaching a stalemate that could destroy the relationship and all hope of helping him.

I then made a decision that I was not going anywhere that day until we had resolved this. I stopped the Car on the side of the Highway and I told him we were not moving untill he came clean. After much persuasion and convincing that I was not going to punish him in any way, he finally admitted to taking it. I asked where it was, and he said in his bag in the boot. So we went and opened the boot, and here is where, in a crucial split second of a moment I got the inspiration I needed, that would achieve everything I needed to teach him - and with proof. As he gave me the money packet, I opened it (which had much more money in than usual) and threw all the money on the highway – even that was an inspiration of where to throw it, because if I had thrown it on the side of the road I am sure he would have picked it all up. You should have seen his face – he was horrified. He could not believe that I had just thrown all that money away. My only words to him were that "you are much more important to me, and this lesson and example is much more important to you and me than the money would ever be" wow – what a moment of triumph.

The lesson closed and we all passed with full marks.

But it did take one more very serious event for him to trust me fully!

Once again, through my having supported him and done all the right things, in something so serious that involved Police and Court, after that I apparently passed all the tests, as he never gave me another problem at all.

It was like he changed into a Teen Angel - and I was also learning, growing, maturing. I was getting wiser at this !

MOON

Oh moon,
magic mirror - that somehow reflects my love,
as I gaze, spellbound by the wonder of your grace
I see all of me
exposed – reposed
basking in the light of your love,
serene – my heart pounds
for now I know I have found,
to you I am bound,
oh magic mirror of my heart.

CHAPTER 17

Disobedience and Consequence - Obedience and Reward

Eye for an Eye! Yes, this is exactly how it is in some cultures – and it works!

We may not need this severity in dealing with our Teens, but the point is it works as a principle because everyone in that Culture knows and so keeps the rules, because the consequence is clearly defined and inevitable, hence it works as an effective deterrent.

You have to make it clear when his behavior is unacceptable – no matter how young the child, they fully understand and appreciate when you make a stand on such issues. You must establish your authority during the informative years – otherwise it is only going to be much more difficult later on. Take heart however – you can start the process at any stage or age, but it will require more resolve from you, and will be harder for the Teen to make the adjustmentthe older or worse condition he is in – but adjust they will, if you are serious, committed and uncompromising.

17.1 It's just so much energy.

It seems that one of the biggest problems in modern day life – with all its demands, pressures and stress – is that Parents struggle to have the time and energy to deal with their Teen on a consistent basis, day in and day out.

Unfortunately, however, it must be that way otherwise it will not work. He will not adjust, and you will be wasting your time and effort, if you are not consistent.

Yes, life has become very difficult, and the demands on our time are worse than ever. Everything seems to be moving so much faster now, so much more to do every day, yet there are still only the same number of hours in each day! After a hard days' work, and the stressful trip home, you are exhausted. Nevertheless, you can't let up. The minute you let go you lose all ground gained over the whole time it took to get to this point! The process is very demanding but very necessary, It will get much easier after you gain control.

You have to commit to the process, and it will be a difficult process, and you have to be serious and determined that you will go for it until you win – not matter what. After all - the life of your Child is at stake – it's definitely worth it. The irony is that the more serious and the more committed you are, and the more they see you will not back down or compromise, the quicker and easier the adjustment will be for him. Read this point again, as it is critical. Understanding it will make your job much easier. Him seeing your commitment will achieve more than everything you can say.

But, as the ADULT – and as the PARENT, it all starts with you. You have to make the decision to do this thing. You have to commit to saving your Child. After all, he wants and needs saving – he just won't admit it openly. He needs saving from himself, from this horrible person he knows he is being, but he is hoping you will make a stand. He has a deep hope you will come to his rescue. He is lost and subconsciously knows or senses it – even if he does not fully understand it all. He desperately needs you as the older one, who should know better – to do something, to correct this situation. Yet he will keep fighting you tooth and nail, fight against all you are trying to do. You have his best interest at heart – but he does not know that, cannot know that until you act decisively enough to show, to demonstrate that you really do care for him. Care enough to do whatever it takes to take the assertive steps needed to save him.

17.2 I discipline because I love.

Love is all too often misunderstood, and then misapplied. Love is not wishy washy – luvy duvy – that won't help you or your Child!

Because I love my Child I discipline him. A good example of how love acts is as follows.

I tell my child not to go play on the road because it's dangerous.

He does not listen, then I find him playing on the road. I give him a warning. Still I find him again on the road. I now give him a hiding, to correct and discipline his behavior, and to get him to be obedient.

He now listens to me and no longer plays on the road.

I have done this because I love him, care for him and want to keep him from danger. His disobedience could have cost him his life! This is how I care for my Child. I do what is necessary for his wellbeing, even if he does not like it, and even if it seems not nice. BUT he will understand the lesson, he will perceive you love and care for him when he sees this caring behavior on a consistent basis. Yes, believe it or not, he will see it as proof of your care. On the surface may react or act indifferent, but he will understand and appreciate this after a while, and it will settle him, and make him feel secure. As this progresses and improves – you will have less and less trouble with him.

If you do not set the stage now, take control and manage your teenager, and bring him under control, you will not be able to do it one day when something more serious or life threatening comes along – then it is already too late!

Just by teaching your child to listen to you when you give instructions, not only makes it safer for him, and more peaceful all round, but he is then also more pleasant to take out visiting etc. We all know there is nothing worse than a child who does not listen to his parents when visiting in your home or out at a Café etc. – he actually disrupts everyone and everything and destroys any pleasant social atmosphere.

17.3 Rules provide a point of reference.

By setting up the rules, and defining them clearly – in writing, you are making a stand. You are showing you are going to take control. You are showing you are serious. These rules will give you the Parent, as well as the Child, the guidelines – or point of reference from which to operate. You will both know where you stand. You will both know what is expected and required. You will both know what the ground rules are for the House. You will both know when there has been a deviation, and this is where you take control, or become the Parent. When he breaks the rule, you apply the consequence or outcome that you have already defined for breaking that rule. This is how you enforce the rules, so that he will start to obey, otherwise he soon learns that he loses out too much by not submitting. This compels his adjustment without severe punishment ever being necessary.

For example – if you make a rule that on a Friday night out, he must be back by 11pm. That is the Rule. Then you must also write the consequence for not following the rule. i.e. If not back on time, next Friday night outing is cancelled, he can't go out no matter how important or what the event. You can make any rule against any allowance/tolerance, but you must also make and define a relative consequence. It is no good to make a consequence for disobedience that he is not bothered about. i.e. no good to say he can't watch TV for 2 nights, if that is not a problem for him. The consequence must be a denial of something he wants, then it will affect him when he can't have it, then it is an effective tool used to correct his behavior. He must start to learn accountability as soon as possible while growing up. If you do what I the Parent want, then I the Parent will give you the Child what you want. If you don't do what I want, you don't get what you want – that is how simple it is. The more he wants something, the stronger that is as an incentive to get him to do what you want him to do, in order for him to get what he wants.

17.4 Kids to work for wants, not needs.

Note that you never do this with his basic essential needs. Those you as a Parent are obligated to provide. Food, shelter, basic clothing, schooling, medical treatment etc. are all necessities.

Fancy or fashion clothing beyond his basic needs are to be earned by working for. He must work for cash, then he must go buy the items he wants himself (with your guidance of course if he is very young) as this teaches them to handle money and teaches them values. If you went out and just bought the item for him, and without him even knowing and understanding what it costs, you have missed a good opportunity to compound the lessons and teach him values.

Just the other day I encountered a young boy casually, and saw he had highlighted his hair. In the interactions I asked who paid and he said his Mother had paid? I told him I would not have, as this was a choice fashion issue, I would have made him pay out of his own pocket money. Now there is no real problem that his Mother wanted to do something for him and paid, but it was a lost opportunity to be a good lesson. This is the type of difference, where, when you make him pay he may think twice about it – as then some of his money is gone – and does he really want it that much to deny himself something else he also wants. Do you see why this becomes such a good lesson in instruction for him. He is now making choices that involve money and values – and so he learns. Once he learns more about value, he will also start to appreciate and to care more for his things. He will look after them much better.

Your Teen should also have an allowance – money – to start to learn to handle money, and to learn the value of money. If you always buy or pay for what they want, they will never learn this lesson. By having an allowance, you have a tool with which to discipline him. If he does not conform, then he may not get any allowance, or may not get a portion of it for this week.

The allowance should not be enough for everything he needs. He should have to do chores to earn more allowance, and then when he does not do his chores this week, he does not get paid. He will quickly learn to do his work around the house. You should also not buy ALL his clothes – as stated already - especially fashion or special items he wants – these should be worked for, so he buys them with his own money – then he will appreciate them more, and also look after them better. This teaches him valuable lessons about work, salary and the value of everything, and prepares him for going out into the big wide World one day (all too soon).

CHAPTER 18

The dreaded 'G' word!

Bobby Griffiths – GAY "Life" gave him nothing but misery and a tragic death.

His life story became a very good, informative and touching epic movie.

Bobby was only 20 when he Killed himself.

Threw himself off a Bridge on the Freeway, in front of a huge Truck! All because his Mother could not accept him being Gay. What a needless tragedy.

Can you imagine what he must have been going through to reach that level of desperation! What a truly sad, sad story, and what a waste of a beautiful young life blossoming to live – and for no better reason than a Parents prejudice (and plenty pride).

I say pride because many parents feel a failure if their kid turns out Gay, they feel responsible and don't want their family and friends to know the 'awful' truth. So they compound his confusion and struggle with lies, deceit and suppression. All this increases his pressure ten fold, and the one person he should be able to run to, to confide in, to hide away in a safe place until he understands better – is with his Parents, or at least his Dad. Unfortunately however, Dads' ego is much too big to deal with his perceived sissy son – and so he goes into denial or rejection of his Son. Shame on you Dad, grow up, he needs you now more than ever, and for his sake get yourself past yourself for a change, and stand by him.

Mothers are usually much more sympathetic and understanding, and far less judgmental. Bobby's' Mother was so profoundly sorry for her Bible punching prejudice, that caused her son to kill himself, that she took it upon herself to find out everything she could about Homosexuality, and ultimately became a renowned Gay activist.

Heaven forbid this Gay boy is in a religious or Christian home – all his problems are much worse due mainly to self-righteous prejudice, compounded by self-bigotry, with guilt and shame that is laid on him for being such a big sinner!

Who is he supposed to go to now? Who can comfort and guide him now? His Dad won't, and indeed can't. His Church won't, and all they usually succeed in doing is convincing him he is so bad, even God won't want or forgive him. The only understanding and acceptance he may find could be in the arms of another man! – or at some Gay Club, where he may be getting all the wrong inputs. But he has to go somewhere, he has to talk to someone. I don't know why it is called the Gay Life, because life is usually hell for him as he struggles to come out the closet. It is incredibly difficult all round for the young Teen, who is just discovering his sexual preferences – which are no choice of his own, but more likely a victim of his environment.

99% of Gays will be able to tell you categorically that it was never a "choice" they made one day. Many would then just choose not to be Gay, and live a happier free life of acceptance and social norm.

Have you ever heard of a straight man choosing to go Gay? this is obviously equally impossible. There are many books written about what makes a boy/man Gay, but few speak much sense on the subject. If truth be known, no one really knows precisely what makes someone Gay. There are some common factors, but that is not the issue for this Book.

He or you just discovered he is Gay, and you need to address that properly from the outset. Your first reaction is critical! If you have already found out, and had already reacted badly – go back to him and say sorry, and tell him you are going to try understand. Tell him you will make a point of finding out all you can, so you can both be reconciled. It is imperative you get to a position where you can help him. Stand by him – he needs you more than ever in this crisis in the Family, but a far bigger crisis for him personally.

If he is Gay, that is that – DO NOT send him to a Psychiatrist or anything like that – you demean him, embarrass and humiliate him – which just alienates him further from you. Start finding out all you can, and start talking to him. Ask him to bring some of his Gay friends home! If he has siblings, obviously you can set up some rules for the sake of the younger ones. Better to know who he is associating with, and anyway, this is a good way to start finding out what's going on with him, and what the Gay scene is all about. This is what will help him, this is what will help him open up to you about where he's at with all this. Remember, his rejection is all around him, not just his Parents!. This is a very traumatic time for him, and he had no guidelines, no help, no hope no support. That is why so many Gays feel their situation is so hopeless that the only way out seems to be suicide.

Men, Fathers who have a problem with Gays are generally insecure about their own sexuality. This is a bold statement, but has much substance. The fact is that when a Man who is totally secure in himself, and especially about his sexuality, he is not at all intimidated about a Gay, or Gays – he has no need to be, and he knows it. He will quite easily accept a Gay friend, or befriend his Brother or Son with little problem, even if he is surprised or ignorant on the subject.

18.1 Mike - drugs, gay sex and...

Mike was 14 when his Dad asked me at 4.30am one morning to counsel his Son who was taking Drugs. …. But Drugs were not his problem, it's was his Dads rejection of him, which made him take Drugs for attention, and even led him into sex with other boys at Boarding School – because he felt why not anyway – my Dad does not care! He was born into a wealthy Family, who owned a large flourishing Business. They lived in a mansion in one of the elite suburbs of Johannesburg. The irony was that Mike was the splitting image of his Father. Like Father like Son! – the likeness was incredible. There was no doubt this was his Son. His Father should have been so proud of him – but nothing could be further from the truth! His father did not want to know him. A Fathers rejection of his Son is the worse crisis a Boy can have. I counseled Mike just by having him in my Home one day a week for a while. I do not believe a professional Therapist can do much for these very serious cases by a one hour Counseling session every week? All the kids I have spoken to who have been through Therapists told me they never told the truth in these sessions. Getting the truth out is a crucial part of the process in counseling, especially if he has thoughts of suicide. You have to get him to open up totally, absolutely and truthfully. This is not easy, and I have had to learn the technique over many years and much experience. The better your relationship has been, the easier this will be. Unfortunately however, the converse is equally true, the worse your relationship has been with him over a period, the harder this will be.

18.2 Gain their trust, and keep it.

I have a unique tried and tested way of achieving this, of gaining his confidence very quickly. I open myself up, I make myself vulnerable, and answer absolutely any question honestly (unless it is info about another person that may be confidential) even then I don't lie, but rather I tell them I am not at liberty to tell them that. I also take responsibility for them and their condition. I doubt this would be endorsed by professional Therapists, and certainly not by Psychiatrists, who generally do not give directional counseling. I DO, and I take full responsibility for the directional advice I provide. They are desperate, they need help, they need to know what to do. I also promise confidentiality, and maintain that – even between the Teen and his Parents – unless it is so serious I feel the Parent needs to know, then I will solicit their approval for me to tell their Parents – but I will not do this until the Teenager trusts me enough to agree. I also make it clear to the Parents I will not divulge anything their Son tells me in confidence. This is an absolute rule I have never broken. This has won the full trust of many troubled Teenagers.

I use various other methods to gain their trust quickly, like body language, focused attention, I listen intently to what they have to say, and read between the lines sometimes. I probe right down into their heart as quickly as possible, before they can get the mental barriers up. Usually within 20 to 30 minutes I have the main story out. From there on it's easy.

I have other tactics once I get them home, to gain their trust further.

Many of them also have to be fed and cleaned up before you can go any further – and even this is made part of the process of gaining their trust and opening them up more and more. You have to gain their trust, and then prove you are trustworthy.

I ask very personal details about themselves, this intimacy also helps, not only the relationship – but in finding out more about them. Once they have answered some personal information (which is not really important to know most of the time) but because it is so personal, they then have nothing else to hide.

18.3 Vaughn

A good example of how well this works was with a runaway boy from reform School. Vaughn, 15, was eventually given to me formally by the Department of Social Welfare. He was also in a reform School, but that was not how we met.

I saw him one evening on the streets of Hillbrow, but he had such a dark cloud over him I ignored him. But then I saw him again, and the third time I instinctively knew he was in trouble and needed help.

I walked up to him – it was already evening - put my hand on his shoulder, and said he had to come home with me! Yes quite bold and a very unusual sort of thing to do, for a Man to "pick up" a boy like this off the streets.

However, I was right – he was totally relieved, as it was getting late, and he said he was on his way to his Gran in Witbank – but had lost his money and clothes, and now had no means of getting there. Of course this was all a lie and I also knew that.

I took him home, and spent the first hour finding out the truth. I knew I needed to contact his Mother, as he had obviously run away from home – or so I had concluded. The truth was he was in a reform school, and had absconded. His Mother was in Cape Town, and when I called her to say I had her Son with me, and that he was fine and that I would get him back to School. She basically swore at me, accused me of abusing her Child, but then said she did not care anyway, and did not want to know anything about him. She had placed him in Welfare years ago already, as she could not cope with a son. He had not done, and was not doing anything wrong, other than that he was Gay – but once again, well adjusted, and not in any conflict over this.

In those days the South African Welfare and Reform Schools were wonderful, and staffed by many really dedicated loving workers.

These Reform Schools allocated a Mother to the boys, also a professional Psychiatrist and a good Teacher to take care of his Education. A wonderful system that worked most of the time.

Now you need to understand that Vaughn being at my house was Technically illegal, he was a Ward of the Court, and I could be arrested for this. As he was in Reform School, and had run away, the Law required whoever found him to hand him over to a Police Station so that he can be returned to Reform School under escort Guard.

I was not having any of that. And in any event, he had begged me NOT to hand him over to the Police as he did not want to be taken back under arrest. I agreed, provided he let me contact the School, and that he let me take him back. He agreed, but only on the basis of when he was ready to go back. I left that timing to my discretion as to when I had won his confidence sufficiently for him to trust me to do the right thing at the right time. I then contacted his Therapist at his School to advise I had Vaughn, and that I was going to bring him back myself, when he was ready. (His School was about 800 Km from where I was living) so this was quite a task. I had to get off work, unpaid leave, spend time and money getting him back, and then more time to get myself back to work.

At this stage I did not reveal who I was or where I was, as the School would be compelled to send the Police to get him. I checked out Vaughn's story with his Therapist, and he could not believe I had the whole story in a weekend, which had taken the Welfare and him two years to find out.! He said I should join Welfare, as I obviously had a gift with these difficult Teens. I would never join Welfare, because my own tactics would never be approved by the formal Welfare structures, and then I could not have as much success with the boys. I told the Therapist I was going to talk to the Headmaster, but that I was going to tell him I will not hand the boy over to the Police. He surprisingly agreed, for the good of Vaughn. He fully understood that I needed to maintain Vaughn's trust, if I was going to be able to help him beyond getting him back to School.

He had tried to commit suicide several times, and was always running away from School with some older Gay guy or other. I needed him to stabilize, and stop this behavior – but there was only a chance of achieving this if I had his full trust, and if I committed to keep supporting him until end of his High Schooling.

I then called his headmaster of the Reform School – he promptly shouted at me and instructed me to take Vaughn to the Police Station immediately. I refused, and then he instructed me to say who I was and where I was. Again I refused, for Vaughn's sake, but did promise to bring back to School personally, as soon as I thought he was ready. He was furious with me, but I just told him I was not one of his school boys, and that I was going to do this my way, and I put the phone down. Thereafter I called him regularly – but always from a public call box so he could never trace me. I gave him updates, and committed to have him back by X date, which at least placated him a little – but he was still not happy with my behavior, but realized there was nothing he could do about it.

This may sound unusual, but one Saturday night at about midnight I sensed God telling me I had to take Vaughn back the next day. This came as a complete surprise to me as I was not sure he was by any means ready to go back – but to my amazement, he was quite happy to go back the next day.

This event and God's direction had a profound effect on my life and changed a very particular bad aspect of my myself. I could never do anything spontaneously easily – I had to plan and prepare, so to be told to take him back tomorrow morning, a Sunday, was a shock to my system, but it cured me once and for all of this idiosyncrasy. I took him back, and His Headmaster became my ally, and often asked me to help him regarding certain boys, or runaways. He told me he never believed I would take all that trouble to bring him back, but when I walked into his Office that Monday, he was very pleased that I had kept my word, and that I had brought his protégé back, safe and sound.

Vaughn went on to finish School and his Education. He never ran away again, and never tried to kill himself again. Welfare formally handed him over to me, so he could come to me in School holidays etc. He was a wonderful boy, and should never have been put in Reform School, but Welfare had nowhere else to put bigger kids, who were too old to place in Foster Homes. Vaughn was so incredibly intelligent, and talented. He wrote Poetry, that he only ever showed me, no one else. At 16/17, he was writing Poems of the maturity of a fully grown mature Adult. Amazing works.

Did the time and attention I gave him save his life? I will never know the real answer to that question – but it is very likely. How could any Parent not want such a brilliant child, He was also very good looking, and had a good physic, and so scored on all points – yet his Mother did not want him. That is what led to his suicide attempts, he felt deep down inside no one cared, no one wanted him – until I demonstrated by my actions that I really did care. That's what reached him and touched him, and changed him.

That's what our Teenagers need. To know they are cared for, otherwise, through normal natural process they feel unwanted and useless.

CHAPTER 19

Suicide

Besides a Gay son, this is probably the most devastating tragedy that can hit a Family. But it does not usually come overnight. There are several factors that can lead to your Child willfully taking his own life – so unnecessarily. I have already addressed the Gay issue as a potential cause when coupled with rejection. However, another very common factor in Teenage boys committing suicide is rejection by his Mother at a very early age. This may only be a perceived rejection, but equally devastating, as it finally takes it's full toll when he reaches adolescence.

I call it the second rejection.

19.1 Mark

Mark was 15, going on 40, and totally misunderstood because he was so advanced in years for one so young. But sadly his Mother did not recognize his maturity, intelligence, high IQ and considerable talents, and just saw him as having something wrong – and in her own desperation to change him, sent him off for Psychiatric analysis! Of course, being so intelligent, he totally led the Doctor down the wrong path and no one could see or understand what was going on.

I wrote a Poem for Mark's 16 Birthday present, which was just after I met him:

MY FRIEND

There is a boy I know
Boy? no
but nearly man
known only in part
yet no stranger to my heart.
Where is he at today?
for it is his Birthday
how many I know not for sure
yet I know it is more.
What can I give him
what can I do?
not to threaten
but to impart and strengthen.
I can't touch him
but touch his heart I must
to reach
to teach.
so myself I will avail
in this I must prevail
for he is my special friend
and no stranger to my heart.

In retrospect this Poem was very insightful and even prophetic, for he killed himself just about a year later.

I think he was the most intelligent and clever person I had ever met in my entire life.

Mark committed suicide just after he turned 17. Rode his motorbike off a Cliff in Pinetown, Durban. They found him on the rocks below, his body a mangled mess. What a waste.

Why, because his Girlfriend broke off their relationship.

But that was not the real reason, no, it was because of his Mother's unconscious initial rejection . Not many Mothers could ever reject their child consciously, but often, due to outside pressures, like a new husband who is not interested in the child, misunderstandings etc, they do reject sub-consciously – but the child is usually fully aware of this. They sense or perceive it long before it comes out.

Before Mark killed himself he wrote me a letter – suicide note they call it. Unfortunately, the Police took it and would not give it back to me, or even a copy, or even tell me what was in it. He did not write to anyone else, not even his Mother and Brother, only to me.

We had written many many very long letters to each other over the last year, pouring our hearts and experiences out to each other. He was honestly like a mature adult, in a Teenage body. He had the mind of a well educated, highly intelligent mature adult – but was stuck in this 16 year old body. His peers did not have a clue about where he was coming from. They were all like children to him – he could never converse with any of his peers. This explains why he got on so well with me.

We met, or rather I met him one Sunday afternoon on the beach, with a beautiful Sunset panorama unfolding, but he was looking away from the Sunset – that's what instinctively alerted me to a problem. The inconsistency alerted me, so I approached him.

He was quite weary of me at first, not sure what I wanted. I sensed this and reassured him as necessary. Within the usual half an hour he had told me his whole story.

I was then focused on getting his trust, so I invited him to go eat somewhere, at a place of his choice, which we did. He was the brilliant mature boy who killed himself with his motorbike a year later.

Mark .... what a waste......

I have had to deal with plenty of suicide and death over the years. You never get used to it, or cope better.

It is utterly devastating, makes everything seem so pointless at the time. Leaves you empty and hurting, with no way to ease the pain or dress the wound, and no one to go to for commiseration. After all I am the Counselor, the Parent, the adult, the strong one, the leader! But it still hurts. It leaves you raw and very tender.

This Poem was written after one of the suicides Funeral.

FUNERAL

The sorrow is for us
as we mourn and weep
and wallow in self pity.
he has no pain
for all is gain
as he is released
oh what peace.
For us who remain
just turmoil and pain
as we struggle on
such ignorance
confusion abounds
all around.
Oh mournful Church
so many sad faces
as they lurch
in their places
no comprehension
only tension
Doom and gloom
here's the coffin
up the isle
not one smile!
what's in the box?
surely not him?
how we hope
as we mope.
Some trick of life!
no, rather the deadly
finality of death
absolute devastation
for all has changed now.
Many tears,

as reality sears the mind
on we move
to the cemetery.
Death is heavy
As six carry the coffin
To the big hole
so deep – so much soil
down it goes
on and on
there he goes, what must I do
my mind reels, my heart tears
it's too deep
how will he breathe
and all that water
curse the rain
he will drown
how can he breathe.
So cold and dark
now he's all alone
not warm in bed
with so much life.
Dead and still.
It's all unbelievable
inconceivable!
what's happening
it's all gone wrong
it's not supposed to be like this
now he's gone
I can't condone
beyond any reach
what will I teach?
My dreams lay shattered
my plans all awry
and so I cry.
He's gone
i'm all alone
I can't condone.

CHAPTER 20

Sex, Affection and Love

The best, and perhaps the only preparation your adolescent is going to get for marriage, is how you relate to them about this subject. There is a direct connection, as he will tend to role play, later when he is married, based on what he saw between his parents. That has set his perception of relationships.

I have seen it time and time again, Parents who have good relationships, have much more stable Teenagers, who grow up into good young adults.

In most cases, our Teens know far more than we realize, and maybe more than what's good for them at this stage. This is especially true about sex, however it is all out of context, as they know little of love affection or commitment. But worse, is that what they know about sex is usually not even the right way – usually no more than peer knowledge – which is very distorted to say the least. If you don't talk to them about affection, love and sex, and the distinction – then everyone else will, and will usually pollute your innocent Child. Even worse, if they know nothing about sex, they don't know what to avoid. They will be naive of all the predators, and will not know what to look out for, and how to avoid such predicaments. This does not mean you must teach your child to avoid strangers, or that all strangers are bad – on the contrary, running to a stranger when in need may save their life?

20.1 Stranded young girl saved by stranger.

Many years ago in Zimbabwe, just shortly after I was divorced, I saved a small lost young girl in a rainstorm. It was just getting dark, and on my way home, as I passed the Convent School gates, I noticed a young teenage girl, huddling by the now closed gates, in a dreadful rainstorm. Of course in those days we did not have the ease of Cell phones etc.

I stopped and asked her what was happening, why she was in the rain, and getting so late, where were her Parents. All she said was she thought they had forgotten her, as they should have collected her long ago. So I told her that she should come with me, I would take her to my home and phone her Mother, and. Of course this was risky for her, but not in Zimbabwe in those days. We never heard of crimes against children like we hear of now all the time. I got her home and tried to call her house but no response. I sent her off to the bathroom to have a hot bath, and gave her some dry clothes that would be reasonable for her to put on.

Once she was warmed up and dry I called again and finally got her mother, who was of course frantic. She had been held up, and got there so late, and found her Daughter gone, she was looking at all known places for her.

Something about her story did not add up. It had been far too late to have just been held up while on the way. Nevertheless, fortunately for the Mother and Daughter, I had handled her appropriately. But what had happened? This is a terrifying experience for a young girl, and probably frightened her for a long time.

But, it was after all, me a stranger to her that had saved her. So there are times when strangers can help – so it's quite chancy to just wipe out all strangers. Teach them appropriately about strangers. Make sure they know their name & No., and especially their Parents name & No.

Yes. Children do ask questions about sex, but mostly out of curiosity, not to study the subject. Also mostly about organs, rather than sexuality itself – of which they are unaware when the questions start. Keep your sex lessons relevant to their age, and the level of questions asked. Don't make the mistake of confusing them by answering much more than they ever asked at that moment. Listen carefully to the question. Check out what they are actually asking, and why / and in what context they are asking the question. This brief will prepare you well for the right level of answer. Careful questioning will also bring out any inappropriate attention they may have experienced, and you can then deal with that and help prepare them, without instilling fear.

Also avoid talking nonsense about Storks etc. If you lie to your kids, as they grow up and realize you have not told them the truth they will tend to distrust you. Furthermore, these lies confuse them as they grow up. So rather, tell them very little each time, but always correct and true, and slowly add more info and more detail as they grow older, until they ask the real questions, and you can fill in the gaps. This builds a steady healthy relevant understanding for them, with consistency. This also prepares them well for their infatuations and their desperate teen 'Love' experiences. Teach them the difference between emotion, infatuation, and when they are ready – lust! Make sure they understand the distinction of love and affection, and how all these fit in with each other. Teach them how and why to keep sex out of these young, innocent relationships, then they will fit in sex properly, when it is the right time, and hopefully, when they are old enough. The most important thing is to keep them talking as these issues progress – and you can keep helping them and keep providing support and more understanding.

Even regarding Death and Funerals, tell them the truth, and this means telling them more, the older they are. Children have a remarkable intuition and awareness, and perceive most situations quite accurately – but then Parents either distort or destroy this ability in Children, by not recognizing it, and then by not responding truthfully. Even financial struggles in the home that many experience at some time or other – get the whole Family together and explain what's going on. Daddy has lost his Job, or his Business has closed down, sales were not enough – whatever - and we will be short of money for awhile. So we all have to cut costs wherever we can. The Family must and will survive, but explain why you need to be penny wise for a while. Children relate to this and understand perfectly. What they can't understand, when you don't confide in them, is all the whispering and stress and lack for no reason at all, and then they start to be difficult about it.

20.2 Let dad answer to boy and mom the girl.

When young children talk about sexual organs in the bath, never stop them, and never chide them. Rather distract them, you may need to provide some simple level of answer relative to their age, but don't make something dirty of it, as that will distort their perceptions, and affect them badly at puberty.

"Daddy why is your Penis bigger than mine" does not elicit a macho explanation of bigger is better, but rather, "daddy is bigger all over, look at how big my arm is compared to yours" This is the right type of distraction, which is still honest, still answers his question, but at the level he is asking. He has no idea of any sexual connotations, so don't give them to your Children before the time.

On the other hand, when you Teenage Boys asks Mom what happened in bed last night, as it seemed I wet my bed, but it was just a little wee? (he may not know about wet dreams yet) He may even say there was some association with a dream of Girls or whatever. This requires a much more careful answer. "OK my boy, we have talked about this going to happen as you grow up, it's no problem, but I think your Dad can explain it better than me – please talk to him about it. Can I tell him what you told me? and tell him you want to come and talk to him? This is to make sure it is not overlooked. This is also respectful for Dad, as it is more his domain (just as a girls monthly period would be more Moms domain, and should be referred to Mom) It is also treating your child and the subject with respect.

DON'T do what my Mother did – screamed at me and told me not to talk about dirty things to her ever again. So of course I did not, and got all the wrong sordid answers as I progressed through High School! This did nothing to prepare me for marriage, and I had more than a few shocks coming for that time (I was totally naïve and ignorant). Of course, other than all the wonderful half-baked knowledge my School friends passed onto me, which created so much confusion, all this info did nothing to prepare me properly for sex even, then as far as love and affection were concerned, I had never heard anything about this, or their role in a marriage relationship. What a shame, I missed the best for all the best years of my life, and in this regard was very unfair to my wife, as she was denied any intimacy at any level for years. We never talked about such things.

I never ever saw my Parents hold hands, kiss or hug!

Sex is the fruit of affection, leading to lovemaking, and Children are the fruit of love – or should be. Unfortunately, all too often children are just the fruit or result of sex.

At puberty boys really need their Dad to tell them what's going on. What an errection is in the morning – no he's not a sex maniac What these raging driving desires are all about. How to contain them, How to understand and deal with them. The door of communication must be open for your Teen to come and talk to you about all these things. You must listen carefully and intently. He needs your focused attention for this, very intimate discussion for him. Be sensitive, be careful, don't damage his enquiries with bullish answers. Answer little until you understand all he is trying to tell or ask you. Beware not to react to any of the questions – no matter how outrageous they may seem. He may just be testing you to prepare you, so he knows where you are at, and how safe it is for him to pop the real question. As your relationship improves you can initiate these discussions. As you are open and frank with him, he will start responding well. I can tell you from experience that it is a wonderful privilege when your boy comes and tells you what happened with him and his girl today! Or when he comes and tells you all his friends took drugs today and he participated. Don't be shocked, don't be angry, be happy he has told you, and respond well, and encourage him to keep telling you what they are doing. Of course you need to warn him against peer pressure, and all the downsides of drugs. Get relevant movies to show him, Movies that depict the tragic outcomes for some of the kids who "try" drugs.

Leonardo DiCaprio was in a Movie when he was very young, about becoming a drug addict – and all the awful consequences. **THE BASKETBALL DIARIES 1995 by Jim Carrol** – watch it with your Teenager, then you can both talk about it, and I assure you, if anything happens with him regarding Drugs, this Movie will be a wonderful point of reference around which to address the issue.

If you need more help, then SANCA in South Africa is probably to most credible organization to provide assistance, and should be successful, as long as he has not progressed too far – if so then the only other help, besides God of course, is the International Organization called "Tough Love".

He needs to know about these things – and he needs to know it from you. This is a very personal and intimate part of a Teenage boys growing up, and I have found over the years, they respond very well to direct talk, preferably in their own lingo, so they actually understand what we are talking to them about.

How do you learn their lingo – spend time with them. Invite his friends over to stay, spend time with them at table, then afterwards alone with them in the garden. Take them out on Hikes etc. at weekends, spend time with them, you will quickly hear all their talk, and they will definitely bring up the subject of girls – good opportunity for you Dad to climb in with some facts and figures. Some good straight talk about girls, boys, relationships, sex and babies. They have to understand – from an adult – that sex is not just about the short thrill, there are many consequences. They need to know what emotions are in all of this. At this age they can't distinguish between emotions and sexual thrills. If they understood a bit more about their emotions, they would not get into so much trouble over sex. They need to know all the outcomes, so they can make more informed decisions about sex and relationships. Regarding all sex, avoidance – in as far as is possible - is the best medicine for youthful relationships.

They need to see affection and love demonstrated at home – especially between Mom and Dad. All this will help prepare them for all the confrontations, temptations and opportunities for sex – the more you have prepared them, the better they will handle it. BUT no matter what they fall into, you must be there for them, you must stand by and support them, show you care for them no matter what. If she comes home Pregnant, you need her to be able to tell you, talk to you both about it, before she does something stupid, that could risk her life, all because she was too scared to tell her Parents. She will now need you more than ever before. Be there for her, that's what she needs now. Not to be judged and condemned or to be made to feel guilty for the rest of her life. Love her, accept her, stand by her and help her. She needs a big hug from both of you so she knows everything is going to be alright.

Affection is a perfect barometer. Is there affection freely between Mom and Dad, Parents and Children. The more affection, the better the home environment. The better the relationships all round in the home, the more affection there will be. Affection can fix many a problem – right there and then. Forgiveness, relief, affirmation, understanding – are all conveyed silently but strongly in affection. A good hug does everyone good. Even your self-conscious son wants and will love the occasional hug. Mom, don't stop kissing him goodnight. Dad, still kiss him from time to time to show you love him. On the right occasions it's very appropriate, but try not in public, he may be embarrassed.

CHAPTER 21

Is there Hope

Well …. is there hope?

Only you can answer that question – because it's really entirely up to you. Your Teens can't address the problem. Your Teen can't take responsibility to correct the relationships in the Home. You are the Adult, it's your responsibility to step up and take the challenge. Be a Parent – get your Home back.

We have all had to do it to some extent, some time or other. All Parents make most of the classic mistakes.

Have you ever watched **"Super Nanny" on BBC?** You need to – she will teach you a lot, through practical demonstration of real live family problems being solved with children.

Two things have always struck me about her programmes and work she does with Parents with delinquent or badly behaved children:

a)   It's always the Parents fault
b)   She corrects the situation within 2 weeks

Once again, I do not say this to make you the Parent feel bad, but to bring you to the realization that it is our fault – because we did not know better, we were doing all the wrong things, just as I did with my first few sets of boys. I have had the God given privilege of having one set of boys after another, over many years. Anywhere from 12 years old – and until they are ready to leave Home and go out to work. This allowed me to learn and correct myself with the next boy, and so on. Most Parents do not have this unique opportunity.

Most parents have one set of kids, then only fond out what they did wrong once it was too late, or when they grew up.

So we have to accept without condemnation that we are at fault. Get over it, forgive yourself or whatever you need to do, for the sake of your child, let it all go, and start again – right from now! It's never too late.

ALL OF ME

For you I would mend my ways
change my days
work all day
come home at night
For you I have searched
all my life
for you I will give
all my life
For you!

We do this because our Child is worth it!

Then the fact that Super Nanny can a stabiles all these Family problems within two week has been my own experience in dealing with teenage boys. No matter how bad they are, what environment they have come from, what circumstances they are in – they can be corrected very quickly. I do not mean all the problems are solved. But what I mean is that the immediate crisis can be turned around, can be corrected or stabilized. This then lays the foundation for building on, for all the hard work it will take to now build a good relationship with your Teen.

It's also very similar to the "Dog Whisperer" Cesar Millan on his TV series. Have you seen how quickly he can correct a problem Dog? Have you also noted that most of the time it was the owners fault? He never condemns or judges the owners, he just exposes them – corrects them, and then teaches them how to handle the Dog properly from then on.

This is what I am trying to achieve with this Book. The difference here is that we are dealing with our Children, our precious irreplaceable Teen – worth more than anything you may own, or will ever own.

CHAPTER 22

The God Factor

No matter what religion or faith your Family follow, and even if the Family does not follow any faith – most of the problems and causes are the same for Children and especially Teens. This is more to do with human nature and the impact the Family environment has on your Teen than anything else.

Whilst most Teens cause chaos in the home – to lesser or greater degrees - it is usually the Parents fault. Either from what they have not understood, and have not done, or because of what they are doing wrong – with all the best intentions in the world.

The most consistent fact is that most Families and most Teens have a struggle at some level – for some time, and mostly to do with their misunderstood needs, or bad communications.

This is not an indictment on Parents, as we were mostly also out of Families whose Parents struggled with their Teen years, and mostly have not been taught how to handle their Teenagers. Most Parents are totally unprepared for and don't even seem to expect the sudden conflict that arises when the pimples pop up!

But my experience to date is that the conflict can be much worse in Christian Homes, because of so many wrong expectations from the Parents.

The proverbial "letter of the Law" seems to be imposed so rigidly, that I think even God is horrified sometimes by our lack of grace, mercy and heart – or to sum it all up 'COMPASSION". It is so easy to become so religious, so self righteous, that we take out all our guilt and shortcomings on our kids. This may be mostly because these Parents tend to consider themselves upright and good living, and God fearing, they somehow expect to have little Angels growing up in their homes. Many times however, nothing could be further from the truth. Children are children, and children become Teens – even in Christian homes, and Teens bring all the usual fears, doubts and insecurities of regular Teems. Because of the contrast in a Christian home, the Teen can be perceived as worse, possibly can even be seen as a little demons! This perspective however from a Parent, only compounds the problem tenfold. The Christian Parent needs to make all the same adjustments advised in this Book, if you want to get your own Child back! If you really want to get him on the right road.

There is no force stronger or more damaging, than forcing the Christian view on the Child, especially when it is a religious dogma or even worse, Christian prejudice, and a distortion of what the Bible really teaches about bringing up your Child. We are exhorted to love our Children, and 1 Corinthians 13, defines that love. Make a check list of all the points on love mentioned, and tick yourself off against which points you comply with – when I first did this check on myself, I was shocked about how few points I could say I comply with! Yet I thought I knew and understood all about love ! How mistaken I was.

I can only speak with any authority on the Biblical perspective, and not on any other religion unfortunately. Lauding it over him from the moral high ground, simply does not work. For Christian families it seems to be worse, as all too often, the Parent throws Biblical quotes at their Teen – which does immense damage. And the stupid statement "what would Jesus do" is so out of all context, and so impossible for the child to comprehend, let alone follow, that this is more destructive than constructive. Imagine how you would handle your Boss bending over you every time you made a mistake at work and asking you "what would Jesus do"! can you see how ridiculous this is, and how impossible it is to answer, let alone comply with. Jesus never did anything wrong, can you say that of yourself – and how much further are our children away from doing everything right. I believe this type of imposition on your Teen will drive them away from God.

This not only discredits the Word of God, but God Himself – as any good Father would never act like that anyway, as it places a burden on the Teen he can't possible deal with, and then creates further guilt, insecurity and internal conflict. This type of inner conflict can be so severe as to drive a Teen to suicide, and you may not even be aware when it is happening, until it is all too late. How would you know, if you are in conflict, and he is not talking to you?

A very good example is **the Movie (A Prayer for Bobby – Mary Griffiths) by Sigourney Weaver 2009.** This Movie demonstrates the issue perfectly, far better than I can ever portray in writing.

Every Christian Parent with Teens, or soon to be Teens need to watch this Movie – it will be a life saver, if you can adapt yourself before it is too late.

NO COMFORT ZONE

Passion emotion
all commotion
can I go on
this way prolong
for I fear promotion
into a deeper potion
of my emotion.
But I must remain
for growth to retain
I must mature
so on I go
come pain or sorrow
I must not refrain
for fear I drain
my life for naught
I must be taught.

I always admire Parents who love and care for their disabled Children. Imagine how much harder all round that must be than brining up our normal healthy children, with no more than just behavior problems? Just imagine the dedication commitment and hardship in all that – what self sacrifice by the Parent – that is love, true love.

According to the Christian Faith, God is Almighty God, Creator of Heaven and earth, and is a loving Father, who set up the whole Family structure to keep order and provide a safe caring home environment for our Children to grow up in. This is why He is so against divorce, as it shatters the children. No matter how well you handle it, divorce tears the children apart. Their Mommy and Daddy should be together, that is their most basic security requirement. God also provided the Manual for life – His Word. The Word of God really is the handbook for life. Have you actually ever read it from cover to cover? Everything you need to know about life, love, family and Business is in there. Once a week in Church, hearing the Pastors Sermon is not going to get you to God, or help you keep your Family together. You are going to need to seek the Lord and His wisdom yourself. You have God's precious gift or gifts of Children, you are to care for them, but He has given us the tools, the info – so it's our responsibility to equip ourselves for this awesome task. It's all in the best handbook ever written – The Bible, the living Word of God, which is also Spirit and Life and Truth. So unlike any other book you read, including this one, which are just words or information. The Bible is different, it is Spirit, so it automatically feeds our Spirit even though we do not know how, and are not conscious of it's work in us "we are under the law of Spirit and Life in Christ".

Then the Word of God is Life. "I will give you Life, and Life more abundantly" Jesus said. That Life He imparts to us by His Holy Spirit is not only energy and strength now, and a better Life, but it also means we already have Eternal Life in us because we are born anew of the Spirit of God, so we are now Sons of God, yes of the most high God!

And the Word of God is Truth. All knowledge will pass away, and ONLY Truth will remain, that is what the Word tells us. His Word is Truth. That means His Word is the only and final Truth on every and any subject. The manufacturers handbook – we need to read it to help our children.

No other opinion can stand against God's Word, as He inspired the Word, and that is why it is the final authority on any matter. We can rationalize divorce, sin or anything, but His Word never changes, His Word is, always was, and always will be the only Truth on the matter.

God says that even the most brilliant idea or intelligence of Man, is just folly to God! (Paraphrased).

Statements like: "Life is Difficult" or "Make the decision and commit to your Child to take control and save him" and the "Word of God" is all and the only Truth.

This is the Christian position, and Christianity is based on the bible, so if you are following this faith – you really need to settle the issue that Gods Word is truth, that you can stand on, and that will give you answers you need.

All these three issues are difficult and create conflict, yet, until we settle them with finality, once and for all that you are going to take each at face value, accept them, and get on with Life, until that point, it just stays difficult and confusing.

We need to settle these crucial issues in us. Only then do we get past all the doubts and conflicts, only then do we transcend the problem, and become part of the solution.

He promised in this same Word of God, "Never to leave us or forsake us" and "if a child asks his Father for a Fish, will he give him a stone – how much more will your Heavenly father give good things to them who ask"

"Ask, and you shall receive, that your joy may be full"

Ask for the help you need.

James 1 says "if you lack wisdom, ask of God…"

We all need more wisdom to help us rear our children better.

As a Christian, your point of reference is your Bible – not every book on Psychology you can find.

CHAPTER 23

It's really easy.

Once you make the decision, and make a stand, it's easier. Yes you can get your Home back, and your own Teen back – back on your side, back operating normally, with reasonable behavior. Back to having a good relationship. Life is just too short to waste the few years we have fighting, stressing and struggling over behavior in the Home. It's actually so easy, I am not going to say much in this Chapter. Here are a summary of some critical steps:

- Pray and ask for God's help.
- Make the decision to bring the desired changes.
- Commit to the decision.
- Muster all the support you can from Family and Friends.
- Make the announcement to your Children / Child. Apologize where needed.
- Start with some very simple basic rules. Write them down. Explain then to your Children.
- Write down consequences for each offence – and impose if rule broken.
- Write down rewards for good deeds, obedience or compliance. Don't forget to reward.
- Get their agreement; adjust until you get their agreement.

- Expand the Rules where necessary, as you feel more confident, and are achieving success, until you have the whole House running smoothly, and with things as you want them.
- Give a reasonable allowance. State what amount and when. Maintain what you promise rigidly. Stop just giving out money at random every time they ask.
- Make them work or do chores for extra pocket money, or earnings. Pay on completion, not next week.
- No more screaming and shouting in the house from Parents or Children. All communications to be civil. If they break this rule, have a consequence, deny something they want. If you break this rule get all the Children together, and apologies. This process will help you to contain your own outbursts. Also they will respect you more.
- Use things they want to be earned for over a period if it is a big item like a PC, I Pod, Bicycle, Cell phone etc (All these items to be age appropriate – and also relevant to their own level of responsibility).
- Make conditions for things they want. Make the conditions clear. Negotiate these conditions with your Child, to gain their commitment to keep their side of the bargain; otherwise they don't get the item they want.

Through all this process start touching and hugging and spending quality time with them. You can't get your Teen back if you don't spend time with them. Show them you care, and are going to do a better job about it, from now on and with their help. You must demonstrate this to be real to them. Words or promises just don't cut it, you already let them down too many times on that score !

Everyone is going to be happier.

Keep on building on these points. Keep on establishing these rules, and these practices. Keep enforcing with no compromise. Yes even when you are tired, or have no energy. If you back down, or slip, they will revert right back to the beginning again, and it will be that much harder second time round, or to regain your position.

Yes, it will all be worth it.
Yes, you can do it.
Proverbs say our Children belong to God. So ask God to help you.
Mom – this is for you for all your hard work!

CHAPTER 24

What's next

Change.

Yes, you have to change if you want to get your own back. It's worth everything you have to do to get your Child back.

I make no assertion that this Book holds all the answers – but my intention is to open the door to all the taboo subjects, you know, those things we don't talk about at Home! Through this process in this book, I sincerely trust I have said enough to make you want to get your Home back! To want to get your own back. I hope I have prompted enough to make you make the decision. To make the commitment to sort out with your Teenager. It's never too late. He wants and needs you now more than ever.

Yes, he may be estranged – even in the same House – but it's still not too late. It may be much harder to reconcile after he leaves Home – but you must still go for it. He is still worth it all.

There is more than enough info in this book to enable you to initiate a solution. Something in this Book will relate to your very own situation. There will be something in this book that will help you kick start this process. Something you never thought possible with your child, has now been exposed, as you are now more aware.

Start anytime, at any level. Work out your decision and commitment first, and with yourself, then go for it. Make sure there is no turning back, no withdrawing. Tell w your Boy what you have decided, and that you will need him to work with you in this, but that you are going to do it anyway.

Both of you. Mom & Dad have to stand together in this.

And it is going to start with some house rules. This is your house Parents, you pay the bills, you are fully entitled to make whatever rules you may decide. And these rules will be followed by the Teen, and if not, there is a consequence to each broken rule. They will be rigidly enforced, come hell or high water. In fact, you as Parent should not even start, until your resolve is firm. Rationalize with yourself how you are going to save him, save the home, save your relationship. Solicit support from each other as Parents – if you are both there. Solicit support from all the children in the house. Tell them things are going to change, tell them the new rules, tell them all must comply at the level the rules are set per age group etc.

Get support from wider Family if you can. If not, make it clear to them in any event, things are going to change, you will start to manage your home and children, and peace will be restored and maintained in the home. It will become pleasant for everyone in the family, and indeed also for your visitors.

Commit to go to whatever length it will take to make an impact and bring the desired change. Make it clear – Your Teens will be required to change their unacceptable behavior. That bad behavior will no longer be tolerated in this house. At every level of non compliance, there will be an adverse consequence for the Teen! He will adjust very quickly. Interestingly, mostly because of your new attitude, especially if spiced with care and affection and better communications from you.

If you don't command respect, you probably will not get it. This will have to come onto the list at some point, once you feel stronger and more confident, make the rule, NO MORE bad language, NO MORE speaking disrespectfully, especially to Mom, and Dad, you need to enforce this. Do not allow any of your children at any age for any reason to speak disrespectfully to their Mother – and certainly don't allow it to yourself Dad.

"Life is difficult"

These famous lines were penned by one of my favorite **Authors – M.Scott Peck** – of course from his renowned **Book – "The Road Less Travelled"**

These are his opening lines – and sets the pace for his Book, which has become one of my handbooks for life and understanding myself and people. I make reference to this basic truth of life – because it is true – but, as he says, until we accept this truth, life is even more difficult.

Until you make the decision and commit to turning your home around – it's going to be nearly impossible – but once you make the decision, and stick to it – it will become a reality because your decision surmounts most of the blockage, whether it be mental, psychological, emotion or environmental – once you commit, everything changes, everything seems to just open up to you, and your mission, from the outset, becomes tangible.

Better to use M.Scott Pecks' own words – they are more descriptive:

"Life is difficult. This is a great truth, one of the greatest truths. It is a great truth because once we truly see this truth, we transcend it. Once we truly know that life is difficult – once we truly understand and accept it – then life is no longer difficult. Because once it is accepted, the fact that life is difficult no longer matters".

I can tell you umpteen more stories about many other Teenage boys and all the dramas, pain and struggle it has put me through. The staggering amount of time and energy over the years, the huge stress and pressure and demand on my time and resources, the many hundreds of thousands in cash (South African Rands) in money I have spent on the boys over the years. Food, clothes, medical treatment, holidays motorbikes, cars, things they have needed, and then all the money I spent doing all these things is way over and above what cash I gave them directly, yet in the end I can still say it was worth it all. Worth it for the lives saved through me and my efforts. This has all been by God's grace and by His help.

Worth it because of the progress many made. Worth it because of them coming through and getting past their problems, coming through to a successful life. Worth it because they were then much more ready to handle the rough hard World they found themselves in through no fault of their own.

Worth it because of all I learned about myself, worth it because of the direct changes to my personality and character, all for the better, as I learned how to be more patient, more tolerant, not to give up with such difficult cases that no one wanted. Worth it as I learned to handle the pain and heartache over many of them and the things they sometimes did that disappointed me and dragged me through such struggles.

Families, Welfare, Schools, Parents and Churches did not want these extreme difficult cases. They ended up with me – and I am grateful for all the benefits, all the fruit in my own life, and most of all because I am now much more enlightened, much more ready to handle these difficult cases. Much more ready to help them better than ever before. Much more ready to handle myself. Much more ready to write this Book, to pass on as much of this as I can for your benefit also.

And above all I have learned more about love, and more on how to love more !

And so with your teen, yes it is difficult, but don't be immobilized by the challenge – take it up, he is worth it all.

What next!

You make the change, you make the decision, you make the rules, you become Boss of your Home and your life.

Get your own back – and start right now!

Just a little interesting tip – make sure you are all eating meals together as much as possible – certainly dinner, this is a very important basic spiritual principle, and will bring huge dividends.

This could be your first rule – and easy to enforce, because if they don't come to the Table, they don't get dinner – they will soon come running, especially Teenage boys, because you know Mom how much they consume every day. They always seem to be hungry.

Now you also be hungry, for change, for a happier better home.

We all want our children happy. It may be appropriate to end off with a Poem of purpose and encouragement:

GROWTH PAST ME

What is the purpose
what is the point
for all this turmoil
for all this toil.
me to break
no – surely to make
the best of me
the better to be.
Is there no easy way
why do I withhold!
must it be pain and suffering?
myself to behold.
Exposure, confrontation agony all
yet I know
this is the only show
where I will grow.
so show me – grow me – do it all
for ready I will never be
but needy yes
oh how I need
to get me past myself.